for Reflections on Retirement

"Having gone through 'Retirement Planning' myself, it seems like it often starts out as interesting, then the task becomes less personal and something I would like to avoid. Dr. Hellkamp's approach turns the focus on something most of us enjoy, thinking about our own past life. By doing so, it provides a source of data we can count on: our own life experience. As a result, we are much more likely to stay actively involved with developing a plan."

Robert G. Meyer, Ph.D.
Emeritus Professor of Clinical and Forensic Psychology
University of Louisville

"We have used Dr. Hellkamp's story with the Sisters of Notre Dame de Namur as supplemental reading material in our Exploring Life Transitions Program. Many of our sisters have found it emotionally and spiritually inspiring and encouraging as they face post active ministry and employment."

Joanie R.F. Gruber, MA., MSW, LISW-S
Coordinator of Office of Life Transitions
Sisters of Notre Dame de Namur, Ohio Province

"Dr. Hellkamp's Reflections on Retirement fills the gap between traditional financial planning that will last a lifetime and the deeper dimensions of life that, together, can build a retirement life worth living… offering personal and enjoyable ways of approaching Retirement, Success, and Contentment. A skilled psychologist who blends personal reflections with research and theory, Hellkamp opens our minds to the power of reflection and the value of critical thinking on the way through our life journey and retirement planning."

John F. Kucia, Ed.D.
Vice President Emeritus
Xavier University

"Having researched retirement a great deal, I was personally done with any planning. Dr. Hellkamp's Reflections on Retirement inspired me to change my mind. Each chapter broadened my vision about retirement planning. Anyone who is looking for an enjoyable strategy for developing a retirement plan should read this book. Anyone who is retired should use this book as a reference to measure their progress in the quest for peace and contentment."

Ed Comer
Director of Psychiatric Services (retired)
School of Medicine, Wright State University

"I have known Dr. Hellkamp as a professional colleague at Xavier University for decades. His book reflects his long-standing interest in the welfare of individuals, especially those individuals who are contemplating retirement or are in retirement. While focusing on how individuals might prepare themselves for retirement, he also outlines steps individuals may take to live fulfilling and meaningful lives as retirees. This well-researched and well-written book makes readers aware of scores of works in various fields, ranging from psychology and history to economics and religion that support his thesis as well as provide suggestions on how to live in the present. As a historian, I highly recommend this book. It is not only informative, but also uplifting."

Roger Fortin, Ph.D.
Distinguished Service Professor of History
Former Academic Vice President and Provost, Xavier University

Reflections on Retirement
David T. Hellkamp, Ph.D. Copyright ©

All rights reserved. No part of this book may be reproduced or transmitted in any form or by any means, electronic or mechanical, including photocopying, recording, or by any information storage or retrieval system, without written permission from the author or the publisher, except for the inclusion of brief quotations in a review.

Published by Cincinnati Book Publishing Cincinnati, Ohio
www.cincybooks.com
Anthony W. Brunsman, president
Sue Ann Painter, executive editor
Kara Thompson, assistant editor
Alaina Stellwagen, assistant editor
Kayla Stellwagen, text design
Paige Wideman, cover design
Kathryn Wright, cover picture
Gregory Rust, portrait of Dr. Hellkamp

Softbound ISBN: 978-0-9772720-1-3

E-Book ISBN: 978-0-9772720-9-9

Library of Congress Control Number: 2020932412

For multiple copies, interviews, and speaking engagements contact: hellkamp@xavier.edu

First Edition, 2020

REFLECTIONS ON RETIREMENT:
Making Aging and Retirement Planning Enjoyable

David T. Hellkamp, Ph.D.
Emeritus Professor of Psychology
Xavier University

How to search for success and
discover contentment in life.

CONTENTS

Foreword	viii
Preface	ix
Introduction	x
PART I – Autobiography: Personal Defining of Success	1
01 Childhood and Formative Years	3
02 Early and Middle Adulthood	19
PART II – Planning Different Areas of Life	29
03 Identity Changes Entering Late Life	31
04 Finances	35
05 Socialization	39
06 Housing Questions	47
07 Health And Wellness	49
08 Importance Of Hobbies	55
09 Maintaining Intellectual Curiosity	57
Thinking Styles	
Informed Visionaries	
Entrepreneurial Vision	
10 Spirituality Issues	91

PART III – Some Final Reflections	97
11 Success Versus Contentment	99
12 Retirement	111
Concluding Remarks	115
References	119

Appendix A
    Live Life For Others: A Letter From
    A Grandchild, Michael Dipuccio
	127

Appendix B
    An Ode To Dr. Hellkamp: A Poem From
    A Doctoral Student, April Sobieralski
	129

Dedication	131

FOREWORD

Anyone desiring to learn about aging and retirement planning will benefit from this work. The brief book overflows with doable ideas and with boundless resources. Dr. Hellkamp explains that preparing for aging and retirement is not an event but a journey that can begin early in life.

What is distinctive about this book are the author's methods, which can be experienced as pleasurable and even upbeat. He relies on simple techniques of self-reflection of his life as a guide to aid others to do a similar self-analysis of their own life experiences to arrive at what success means for them. Once the meaning of success is clarified for oneself, Dr. Hellkamp explains how one can identify self-passions and then develop goals across different areas of one's life, especially when planning for retirement years.

Dr. Hellkamp always approached his professional career (and we now learn his personal life) with a uniquely focused energy and dedication. His influence has extended beyond the classroom, not only reaching his students, but his colleagues, associates, family, and the public. I can't wait to share this wisdom-filled book with friends, relatives, students, clients, and colleagues.

Robert E. Wubbolding, Ed.D.
Professor Emeritus, Xavier University
Director, Center for Reality Therapy

PREFACE

REACHING RETIREMENT AGE means, among other things, a person has been plain lucky because one's life was not cut short by a fatal accident, war, someone's vengeance, one's own questionable judgment, or some terminal illness. Yet reaching elder status is not a journey most people eagerly pursue. Our culture still places a premium on youthfulness. Then, one day, having passed all the "luck" tests, you continue aging until the time comes when you become a retiree!

Although retirement includes its share of mounting losses and challenges, usually within health, financial, social, and identity areas of life, it can also include its share of enjoyment and success. It is my assumption that achieving success in the aging process is related to solid preparations. Such preparations, combined with other coping factors, can allow individuals to grow and succeed throughout the life cycle into retirement and discover contentment along the way.

By presenting a practical psychology for coping with the aging process, based on a personal self-analysis, one can learn to prioritize planning for one's own life journey, especially maturing into what is usually called retirement. Using reflections of your life as a tool, you can develop an enjoyable, freeing, clarifying, and positive vision for your plan. Your *mission* is to seek a successful life journey into retirement, discovering a soothing contentment along the way.

DAVID T. HELLKAMP

INTRODUCTION
An Important Objective of the Book

Rationale for this book. At the time of completing this book, I turned 79 years old. I began this work two years ago when a former colleague (Zucchero, 2017) asked me to write a brief paper about "Success Factors and the Aging Process." The plan was to identify seniors they viewed as aging successfully and ask them to write retrospectively about their experiences. My preliminary writings were published in blog form in two parts (Hellkamp, 2017a; Hellkamp, 2017b).

I decided to expand the paper for several reasons. The first reason stemmed from reviewing an invited commencement address I prepared and delivered to the graduating class at Xavier University in 2012. That address also pushed me to examine some success issues related to my personal life and professional career as they might relate to the life journey ahead for the new graduates (Hellkamp, 2012).

The primary reason for expanding the paper was based on two curious facts: (1) demographic statistics indicate that elders will continue to become a larger base in society, and (2) it is estimated as little as ten percent of elders have done much serious planning preparing for aging and retirement. The central question becomes… why are most people not planning, especially considering the number of retirees is increasing and retirees can expect to live another 15 years post-retirement on average? Perhaps, in part, retirement planning is not an enjoyable experience for many, in other words, a turnoff! Maybe the focus needs to be on trying to make planning a more enjoyable, appealing process.

The current book adds the dimension of self-reflection about one's own life and how it can become the basis for developing a plan leading up to and preparing for getting older and, eventually, moving into retirement. My hope is a more complete discussion about successful retirement planning will supplement the literature about how to plan and adjust successfully for one's final season in life. Therefore, I will walk you through a method for self-reflection based on my life journey that can demonstrate how you may extract planning ideas by evaluating your own personal life history and experiences, while learning to enjoy and be inspired by the process.

Professors have focused on retirement in the past. Over twenty years ago, a book titled, *Professors Talk about Retirement* was authored by Dorfman (1997), providing a rich data source of reported experiences and, by implication, suggestions for retiring successfully.

Most importantly, by reviewing hundreds of books and articles that had been published about retirement planning, I found most focused primarily on financial planning, disappointedly, not discussing the many other areas of life that also need attention when planning for different stages of aging, late life, and successful retirement.

Before I begin, I should emphasize that I strongly believe entering retirement is no different from transitioning into any previous, earlier stage of life, at least from the standpoint one must reasonably prepare for it in order to more likely experience success. Success can be defined in different ways. For many Americans, success is defined by achieving money, power, and fame. After self-reflection on my life, I defined success for me as primarily looking inward past pure cultural expectations with the aim of trying to do good things and inspire others, to enhance the common good.

Any money, power, or fame that is achieved is secondary, icing on the cake.

My way of defining success was constructed through a rather simple self-analysis of my personal history, especially family background, by identifying values and priorities that formed the basis of what success might mean for me. Once the meaning of success was identified, I found I was in solid territory for how to plan many areas of late life and retirement.

I can't emphasize enough how fortunate I feel to be living a full life. For me, experiencing a full life is a blessing and, surprisingly, adds greatly to accepting the ultimate paradox of life, inevitable illness, and death. This final chapter in my life is being experienced in a more clarifying, wholesome, freeing, yet questioning way than I anticipated when I was younger. I am generally enjoying this stage of life, but, certainly, in age-appropriate ways that are different from previous stages.

I might add, maintaining a sense of humor can certainly be a very valuable asset, especially at this point in life, to help deal with the mounting losses one experiences. Additionally, some advances, especially in technology and communications, allow us to stay connected to and interactive with persons, information, and events, thereby contributing immensely to the enjoyment and continued participation in the world around us. Sadly, many retirees experience too much isolation and loneliness.

I do believe developing a reasonably clear vision for your journey into retirement is one key element leading to a successful retirement. Due to the increasingly fast pace of change in this world, a built-in flexibility in one's life planning will also be necessary. Such a planning process

INTRODUCTION

would assume more people need to embrace the fast pace of change in this world with positive passion and integrity, not anxiety, fear, or other negative feelings.

Admittedly, my views are only one perspective among many. Perhaps all perspectives will lead to more informed debate and discussions about various developmental issues regarding success and contentment during aging and retirement.

A final observation about my experience in writing this book. Although it began as a rather innocuous endeavor focusing on describing success factors and the aging process, as I decided to expand the topics leading into retirement, it became much more personal. The use of self-examination about one's own life history is more than just a project for others to read; it also becomes a very personal project for the planner. In my instance, it became not only a description of my life planning into retirement, but also a description of many aspects of my life as a person.

In some ways, prior to writing this book, I, perhaps like many other retirees, would have described my past life as consisting of different segments of a long journey, something like a puzzle, sometimes appearing to lack continuity or a storyline. The project was "forcing" me to integrate and make some sense from all the available facts and memory pieces in my life story. In that way, I was able to bring greater clarity to my life, not only having relevance for entering a successful retirement, but also, as a written legacy for family and others.

The whole process was usually exhilarating and enjoyable, but sometimes confusing, sometimes very mundane, and sometimes painful. The reality is, if one is being authentic, one must not only deal with success experiences in one's life, but also relive some of the failures and hurt, in addition to some periodic lapses in judgment and behavior. I'm sure anyone who has written an autobiography knows these dynamics, including dealing realistically with some memory bias, distortions, and ambiguity along the way. Overall, it was still well worth the effort.

Thanks to the wisdom of our founding fathers in establishing a structure of government that, ideally, allows us to experience greater individual and group freedoms, most of us should be able to develop our own personal roadmap for planning our life journey into retirement. Our retirement plan can potentially include whatever our talents, imagination, and opportunities will permit. In that way, planning and experimentation with all that life provides and throws at us becomes possible. The same is true during retirement years.

Relevance for the Reader. I believe it is never too early or too late to prepare for a more complete and fulfilling life in the aging process and during retirement. Think of it as a way of giving yourself permission to step back from your everyday life duties, preoccupations, and pressures to take a look at the larger picture that can impact your own journey, especially with achieving success in your planning process.

Please note as I begin telling my life story, my goal is to share how success was defined for me in my family during childhood and later. A basic tenet of this book is that success is defined differently for each of us. Early on, our family has a subtle, but strong influence on us. It is important to become aware of our own family's way of molding the meanings of success for us. As we move from early to middle and into late adulthood, our societal culture plays more of a role in both refining and further defining success for us. Perhaps for many of us, our childhood experiences are most influential, even though we may have seldom focused on it.

In telling my life story in historical form, my goal is to show how these early personal meanings of success played out in my life leading into retirement. By also sharing my life and success experiences across different regions of life, my goals are to aid the reader to become aware how the experiences of success and contentment were discovered and played more and more of a central role in my life, especially how it influenced the planning process.

You might follow a similar process to develop your own planning. Please note, if you are under 50, it is not necessary to conduct a detailed personal or autobiographical self-examination of your past. What is ideal would be to begin as early as possible collecting background information, family and otherwise, and keep it all together in a container or files. This could include writing down your significant life experiences (personal, social, educational, and vocational), keeping letters, pictures, and anything else, and maybe participate on occasion in discussions (maybe recordings or whatever technology permits) with friends, colleagues, siblings, cousins, and older generation family members. Many people have already kept much information for nostalgic and family legacy reasons. Now you can add to the data for the purpose of successful retirement planning. If you would like additional help in capturing facts, memories, and meanings of your life experiences, I would refer you to the brief book by Franco and Lineback (2006), titled *The Legacy Guide*.

At a later age, you would then have ample information available to begin sketching a personal or autobiographical analysis of your life. Using reflection or self-examination as your tool, you would be able to fill in greater specifics and connections as to the meaning success (had) has for you. You will also be in a position to reflect in an informed manner about your journey in different areas of life. At first glance, this may seem like a lot of work, but, in reality, it is not. It is done in bits and pieces over time.

Keep in mind, you are never being asked to *write* out your own autobiography such as was done in this book, although I suspect some will. You are merely using background information, likely developing an outline of your life and integrating your journey in your mind, maybe following a process similar to the one in this book. You will then be in a better and more accurate mindset to identify your life and retirement goals. You can allow yourself to think more systematically about your passions that are meaningful to you. All of this reflection should allow you to further identify and elaborate key elements for your retirement plan.

Retirement planning differs from one person to another. Overall, retirement planning can be a very personal process, not something one usually discusses with just anyone. During the process, do not be sidetracked by thoughts that you wish you would have done this or that in a different way as you think about the past. Stay focused as to where you are, regardless of any past decisions you either liked or did not like, and strive for establishing goals reflecting passion as to where you wish to go.

This entire process can become more condensed the later in life one starts the process. But, by no means, is the task

INTRODUCTION

that complex or impossible. This method makes psychology work for the typical person by telling your own life story! What it can do is ease the transition into retirement, leading to clarifying a plan along with earning contentment along the way.

I hope my experiences and observations about success, contentment, and other issues I discuss about life and retirement will be relevant to many different kinds of reflective readers. Maybe many more people will become active and begin planning for aging and retirement.

Therefore, apart from a general readership, I would hope this small book might be used as supplemental reading by health care workers and other facilitators, such as teachers, physicians, psychologists, social workers, counselors, financial advisors, human resource personnel, mentors, and life coaches, with adults of all ages. Perhaps my book will also resonate with certain organizations who look to improve their role in helping their members (employees, staff, students, alumni) plan and look ahead to major life transitions, especially later life, and retirement.

In summary, the ultimate effectiveness of this personal, autobiographical approach using self-examination as a tool will not be measured by following a "cookbook" recipe. You must rely on the unique qualities within yourself to record your own historical moments and decision points, to be open with yourself as well as being creative and intuitive. Then examine all areas of life important to you at the appropriate times. Although I have identified areas of life that were important to me, you may identify some other areas of life important to you.

In such a way, you will maximize the likelihood of success in developing an identifiable roadmap for both retirement planning and meaningful living as a retiree. Keep in mind, parts of your plan can change during both the pre-retirement phase as well as during the retirement period due to unexpected opportunities that occur for you. Being prepared for meaningful change is an important dynamic at any stage in life.

The book is organized in three major parts followed by concluding remarks, references, appendices, and a dedication section. Part I focuses on the construction of my personal analysis or autobiography for the primary purpose of helping identify the meanings success had for me, demonstrating a model that you might use to construct your own life history for identifying what success means for you. Part II highlights different areas of life that were important to me to consider in the planning process, including retirement planning. Finally, Part III elaborates on additional meanings of Success, Contentment, and Retirement.

After reading my ideas, it will be your turn to focus on your own life story to identify what success means for you and to begin (or broaden) your own planning process.

PART I

Personal Analysis - Autobiography: Searching For One's Own Meanings Of Success

October 19. This date is Yorktown Day, a fact not many people know about. It is significant because Lord Cornwallis surrendered at Yorktown, a surrender that ended the American Revolutionary War. Unlike Yorktown, most of us easily remember the 4th of July as Independence Day. Truly, we all remember things for many different reasons. Sometimes we remember what we want to remember, see what we want to see, hear what we want to hear. We all don't remember, see, or hear the same things. By telling ourselves and each other our stories and memories, including what we see and hear, we can learn, remember, and do more. So, I welcome the opportunity to share my life story with you. Hopefully, you can learn more what success means for you and move on to plan your own life story for aging and retirement.

DAVID T. HELLKAMP

Read, learn, and be inspired to plan.

CHAPTER 01
Childhood and Formative Years

Experts tell us our personalities, including our potentials to mature and succeed, are based on the interaction of our genetics, early formative life experiences, opportunities, and self-drive. I believe it is important to examine one's own family background as best one can to help determine how success was emphasized early on for oneself. Throughout my personal background and autobiography, I will point out the meanings of success that influenced me and were internalized into my life. I have italicized many of the success components (values and priorities) emphasized in my life throughout the discussion in the chapters, especially the first two. How one defines success for oneself will influence, probably strongly, how you go about preparing for different life stages, including retirement.

Family Background. I was born October 19, 1940 (Yorktown Anniversary) in Cincinnati, Ohio to second generation parents whose fraternal parents each immigrated from the region of Oldenburg, Germany (ancestry.com). On a visit to Germany in my later adult life, the Oldenburg area and elsewhere, I was able to meet many of my living relatives on the fraternal side of the family (Hellkamp, Deekin, and Meyer). With the help of a German cousin and her husband, we were able to trace the family tree back to the late 1400s, discovering that early Hellkamp relatives lived and worked as farmers, homemakers, law enforcement officers, politicians, teachers, and entrepreneurs. The earliest were likely farmers as the German origin of the name Hellkamp is "hell" (bright or sunny) "kamp" (fields), considered the best land for farming.

In speaking to several cousins and others from my mother's side of the family (Wuest), I was able to trace back several generations as well. My mother's father was both a tailor and clockmaker. His passion, maybe obsession, included being an artistic woodworker, making, among other things, clocks with numerous moving parts, such as the Last Supper of the Lord, similar to a simpler cuckoo clock, but extremely elaborate and of museum size and quality. A few other stories were conveyed to me, all with an overlapping theme of how *success* was defined in the family. Simply stated, *one should work to achieve success by emphasizing excellence,* a theme certainly carried forward by my mother to us.

As to birth order, I was the youngest of four sons, my three brothers ranging from six to ten years older. As a result, most of my memories of childhood included growing up as an "only child," as all three brothers joined the Navy upon graduating from high school and were involved in the Korean War. Their friends were not generally in my circle of friends. Consequently, even in the years before they left, we did not "hang out" together.

In another family dynamic, three of my grandparents were deceased before I was born, the fourth right before I turned two. Consequently, I have no personal memories of them, leaving a huge void in my early personal experiences of *what having grandparents can really mean in one's life. I remember wishing I could somehow rectify the situation!*

My father, Edward, became an electrician early on and was either the first person, or one of the first, hired at the new General Motors automobile plant that opened in Norwood, Ohio in 1923. He later married my mother, Elizabeth Wuest. Her father was married four times! The first two times were in Germany. No record of what happened to the first wife could be found. It is likely she died young, some conjecture during childbirth. His marriage to the second wife ended in divorce in Germany during WW1. The third wife reportedly died in America, while his last wife was the younger sister or half-sister of the third wife, and my grandmother. My mother and her brother were twins. I was told a total of 15 children were born to my grandfather Wuest. *Being part of a large family was experienced as a comfort for me.* Many Wuest cousins remained close to our family.

My mother's role was mostly a stay-at-home wife and mother. Dad was frequently away from home traveling during my early years. For a brief period of time during my preschool years, I remember my mother had health problems, which required her to frequently walk the quarter of a mile to her doctor's office for her appointments. I learned much later in life she was likely experiencing panic attacks. Since I was of preschool age, she would take me with her on these occasions.

Early Formative Years. On one such early occasion, she slipped on ice and fell. Being under five years old, I remember being scared and worried because she was bleeding. I "successfully" helped her get to the doctor. *I vividly remember believing I was somehow responsible to make sure she would arrive safely for her doctor appointments after that incident.* The experience passed, but not my memory of it. Maybe not by coincidence, *I was later drawn vocationally to a helping profession.*

Regardless, Mom always welcomed my friends into our home. She was very religious and disciplined. Like many women of her generation, she had the opportunity to earn little formal education (sixth grade). Nevertheless, *education was always a high priority in our family culture,* not always reflected solely in "book learning," but by teaching us *how to notice and be intrigued by wider issues around us.*

For example, a vivid early memory (1945) from my childhood was a simple, but exciting observation one dark evening in the backyard with my father. It was a clear night and he had me focus on the bright moon in the sky. He pointed out his hidden desire to be able to travel to the moon, but recognized that it would not be possible for him or his generation. He believed strongly that humans would travel to the moon in my generation. Through that experience and other similar observations and inquiries, my parents engendered in me a lifelong curiosity about not only *what is,* but *what can be...* a strong appetite for intellectual curiosity. *Success became associated with intellectual curiosity.*

Early in his work life, Dad helped organize the automobile workers union in the Norwood plant, the United Automobile Workers (UAW 674) and served as president and a board member for many years. Through such efforts, he networked both regionally and nationally with the UAW/CIO and many other major union organizations. I remember meeting John L. Lewis, president of the coal miners' union, and Jimmy Hoffa, a later president of the Teamsters, as well as other union leaders of historical note, not having any idea about the role unions would play in the expanding economy. Only later did I learn about their impact on workers, helping create the USA's "greatest generation" (Brokaw, 1998). Among other factors, the middle class then participated maximally in the economy's distribution of wealth, so different from today's middle class.

I believe that Dad maintained the highest "seniority" status at the GM plant even though he focused on the UAW activities, among other leadership roles, throughout most of his working life. He had a strong sense of helping the underserved and mistreated, being publicly recognized for such on numerous occasions later in his life. This belief in *social action, "having the back" of workers and serving the underserved,* was a strong value imbued in our family ethics, also a measure of success.

My first dozen or so years involved growing up in a town adjacent to Cincinnati called Norwood, which consisted of approximately 35,000 residents at the time (Mersch, 2006). *A strong sense of community existed, as most neighbors knew each other, trusted each other, looked out for each other, and shared similar goals, such as upward mobility for their children.* My family can be described as lower middle class, struggling financially on occasion. *The neighborhood values became ingrained.*

My brothers and I later became aware we assumed significant cultural privilege by the mere fact of being white and male during those times and as we matured. During this period of my childhood, birth through 6th grade, all my school friends and those in the immediate neighborhood were white, with little diversity of any type.

The lack of diversity was a different experience from the one I experienced at the school I attended for the 7th and 8th grades. In those last two years of grade school, I became exposed for the first time to cultural, racial, and socioeconomic diversity in a way I hadn't experienced before. This was an eye-opening time for me in that I became aware "equality" was not the same for all... a subtle but profound cultural reality that continues in subtle and sometimes not so subtle ways even to this day. As I look back, I realize I internalized *the value of equality as another component of success.*

My father took every opportunity to educate himself since he earned only a high school education. He ended his work life being appointed by the Governor of Ohio, Michael DiSalle, as one of three judges to serve on a State Appeals Panel, the Ohio Bureau of Unemployment Compensation Board of Review, whose purpose was to make final arbitration decisions for any employee-employer dispute being challenged anywhere in Ohio. Coincidentally, he became an invited guest speaker at Xavier University and elsewhere, on occasion, due to both his Union and Appellate experiences.

Consequently, in the family, besides a value on education, we were also taught to give achievement a high priority. *Success in my family was defined through achievement, self-growth, and leadership while doing good for others, especially in areas emphasizing benefits for the vulnerable and underserved.* I also remember one of my early teachers using on several occasions the word "serendipity," a strange word at the time, defining it as *"chance (success) favors the mind that is prepared."* She would further add, *"Relish change, do not hide from it!"* The statement had little meaning to me at the time.

Later in life, I discovered my mom and dad went through some very stressful periods during my early years, both financially and personally, but were always able to work the problems out. Consequently, I always felt safe and protected at home even during those early trying times. Some of the neighbors, especially "my second mother, Schnetzer," as I knew her, including several of my aunts, uncles, and cousins, remained very close. The Catholic Church also played a major role in my early family dynamics.

In other words, *a very protective network of people around me provided guidance, support, love, mentorship when needed, coupled with attitudes fostering the values of achievement, education, and upward mobility.* All these factors were considered as essential background components contributing to both my opportunity to succeed as well as how I might set my goals to achieve success. Looking back, I was a very lucky dude having such family and social support.

Teenage Formative Years. My oldest brother, Don, was the first in our family to graduate from college. He became a teacher, coach, and administrator in elementary, secondary, and adult education schools in Cincinnati and throughout the country. He was innovative in teaching methods in many programs. To this day, even though retired for many years, he will yet become very passionate about "educational reforms" he believes need to be implemented in our primary, secondary, and adult educational schools.

I didn't know until later in my life that Don was also responsible for my applying to the Jesuit high school in Cincinnati, selling my parents on the idea my best secondary education would be gained at that school. I'll never forget the day in the 8th grade when the principal barged into the class to inform me in front of everyone, I was accepted into St. Xavier High School, something she was no doubt proud of, but one of the worst days for me of that school year. None of my school friends would be attending St. Xavier High School.

This was a repeat of my experience socially two years earlier when my parents had moved from Norwood to Colerain Township, requiring me to spend the 7th and 8th grades in a new school where I knew no one. All my early friends were left behind, a very lonely and challenging experience for me.

In hindsight, *those experiences taught me the hurt of losing friends, the need to experiment with making new friends, and, more generally, the importance of having to learn ways to cope under such conditions* with early teenage stress.

Little did I know at the time, my introduction to Jesuit education, beginning in 1954, would serve me well until the day I retired from my work life as a professor at a Jesuit university (Xavier University) in 2012. Even more ironic is the fact that my home in Norwood (the first 12 years of my life) was only approximately one mile, as the crow flies, from the Xavier University campus, where I also attended college.

Both other older brothers also went to college or technical schools. Each eventually purchased and headed his own business until he retired. Dick, my second oldest brother, and his wife, Marge, had four children. Later in life, Dick bought and developed an electric company in Raleigh, North Carolina, while also earning a law degree.

Larry, after starting as an X-ray technician, advanced into administrative roles at several local hospital radiology departments as well as the Duke Medical Center in North Carolina. He was also innovative, such as in developing a low-dose X-radiography for which he was later honored. He and a son started one of the first mobile CAT-Scan businesses, which became very successful. After Larry sold the company to his son, he turned his work efforts to purchasing and maintaining a large fishing resort named "Southern Komfort" on over 200 acres located on the Kentucky Lake in Western Kentucky. Larry loved the outdoors and followed his dream by running the resort for almost 30 years. His wife, Rita, and several of his kids also helped.

As I grew older, I realized *each brother helped teach me differing aspects of entrepreneurial activities.* In addition, all of us became *"social activists"* in certain areas of our work and/or personal lives. Apart from having seven children, Don and his wife, Jeanne, took in and raised two other kids in great need as though they were their own.

Larry had ten children in two marriages. When running the fishing resort, he would hire indigent persons, frequently with special needs, to work at the resort while attempting to rehabilitate them. I received many phone calls from him over the years to inquire what recommendations I might have for helping them.

As to my academic development, I did not excel grade-wise (book learning) in high school or my first year as a college student at Xavier University. Then, a twist of fate happened. Dad took the Appellate Court job in Columbus, Ohio. Instead of my leaving home to go to college, my parents left me. I was forced to find living quarters on campus at Xavier!

During that time, my second year, academics became very important to me for the first time on a sustained basis. The "fire in my belly" was lit, especially by several professors who took a special interest and became mentors for me. *I'll never forget the importance and impact mentoring had on me.* I believe success for me also came to include providing mentoring for others, a kind of giving back. *Mentoring became associated with teaching, intellectual curiosity, and research.*

My grades went from Cs with an occasional B, to mostly As and Bs. I originally chose a major in math and physics mostly because I always seemed to do well in math and the sciences. In my second year of college, I signed up for a general psychology course, which was mandatory. There I was exposed to a new professor at Xavier with a funny name, Dr. Vytautas Bieliauskas.

I became fascinated with both the class and the professor. I also discovered I did not experience any solid passion for physics or the other natural sciences, especially the labs, as I found them too impersonal. Psychology, on the other hand, emphasized learning about human behavior, a personal and more intriguing subject for me. Psychology also used a math foundation, but mostly specialized statistical formulas and analyses. It felt right as a major. It was a solid decision, not a decision by default. But wait, I get a little ahead of myself.

If you remember, I had no sisters in my immediate family. My mother was the only female. Neither of my parents would be described at that time as warm and fuzzy personalities who freely expressed affection or spoke openly to me about personal issues. In effect, I learned very little about the emotional needs and manners of the opposite sex.

During early teenage years, I was pretty much left on my own in that part of my life. Girls were of strong growing interest to me, but in many ways, unknowns to me. In retrospect, I did not do overly well or handle early male/female relationship issues very well. I experienced myself as very shy and failing in confidence around girls. As a matter of fact, if it had been a school class instead of street learning, I would have probably failed the course at worst, or earned a "C" at best!

Two of the first girls I was drawn to, each in a more platonic manner, one in the 4th grade, and the other in my junior year in high school, joined the convent! A stunning coincidence I now think! Adding to my situation during my teenage years, both my high school and university were gender limited, for boys/men only. The few female relationships I pursued during those years included not only attraction and dating, but also very fundamental sexual curiosities and experimentation.

As a result, I ended up marrying at age 19, due to an unplanned pregnancy. I was very naive and it was the era prior to the acceptance of the pill, or birth control generally, especially within Catholic beliefs. In retrospect, in a perfect world, I would not have chosen to marry or become a parent so young. But it was not a perfect world. I loved my wife and became excited about our new and suddenly changed lifestyle.

Entering Adulthood. In our own ways, I believe we attempted to make the best of it during those early years. However, over time, our marriage endured increasing complications. As it turned out, the best part of the marriage early on was our relationship, while in the long run, it was the six children born. The major advantage of having a family while very young was that I was still "young" as they grew into teenagers and young adults. I was able to do many activities with some of the kids, such as sports, to not only coach them, but also to play on teams with the older ones. Also, *I am able to know my grandchildren and great-grandchildren.* What a wonderful aspect of family success.

I continued college full time and completed my BS degree in psychology. I worked three part-time jobs while attending to school and family matters. Besides the major in psychology and a more general liberal arts education, I had two minors: one in philosophy and one in economics. Philosophy taught me *the importance of values, especially what is called today social justice,* and how to begin using *"critical thinking* skills" as a necessary form of *problem solving and seeking truth.*

This was at the beginnings of the 1960s, a period in American history of great social and political divisiveness and unrest, primarily focused initially on the Castro revolution in Cuba, then race and gender equality issues, the assassinations of the Kennedys and Martin Luther King, the Vietnam War, and finally, in the '70s, on political and presidential corruption (Watergate).

Many in my generation began experiencing on a collective basis that social justice should be more than words. Protests in most major cities and on college campuses included violence, destruction, and sometimes loss of life. We learned the *potential value of protests in an open society, while also learning freedom should never be taken for granted.*

As a side note, social and political protests are again occurring after almost 50 years of relative absence. The Trump Presidential era has highlighted much social divisiveness and unrest that I have not experienced or witnessed in our country since the 1960s and 70s. Among other factors, a break with traditional American political, economic, and social values, along with a devaluing of government and social structures (Congress, the judiciary, the free press, coupled with alleged greed and corruption in the executive branch) are considered by many as major symptoms of this unrest.

Such periods of social and political unrest are not by chance, as economists, sociologists, and historians have documented. Economically, American society was transitioning from an agricultural society to a manufacturing society in the second half of the nineteenth century when the Civil War occurred, and from a manufacturing to a service society during the middle and latter part of the twentieth century's upheaval. Today, we are experiencing another major layer of change into a computerized, digital, technological society coupled with a major energy transformation from fossil fuels to green energy with initial signs of serious man-made climate changes.

Each of these changes redefines many behaviors of people through major power shifts in society (Toeffler, 1990; Maddow, 2019), while disrupting, at least temporarily, many values, ideals, and relocations of people. The American "experiment" has been able to withstand such disruptions in the past, and is again being tested mightily. I do remain optimistic.

Philosophy, especially epistemology, also taught me *the different avenues that can be used to arrive at truth,* such as science, law, theology, philosophy, investigative journalism, and more informal common-sense methods. Just as important, I was introduced to an understanding of what can be concluded when seemingly contradictory "truths" are deduced from two or more of the methods of study. I learned how important it is to review extensively each of the different methodologies that were being used in arriving at the "truths."

For example, scientific evidence overwhelmingly supports the theory of evolution, whereas some literal religious interpretations of aspects of the Bible could support the theory of creationism. I learned why these different "conclusions" do not need to be viewed as an either/or "truth" situation, and how each "truth" can be understood, evaluated, and acted upon. Most importantly, *obtaining truth became associated with success.*

In a much different way, the minor in economics taught me about our economy, about such things as the different complexities of money, credit and debt, banking, the role of the Federal Reserve, business cycles, the "free market," distribution of wealth, and fundamentals of investments, such as within the stock, bond, and real estate markets. As time went by, it greatly aided in my understanding of why recessions are a recurring part of the economy. More practically, I learned that if you are to achieve success, you must act responsibly. *Acting responsibly included learning it is important to plan ahead for "difficult times," not just the good times.* This was a strong lesson for success.

As I began my senior year in college, I discovered another possible vocational passion as well: *the possibility of going to law school* rather than graduate school in psychology. In the end, I decided to work full time on a master's degree in psychology following completion of my bachelor's. Being married by this time and having two children, I engaged my full-time graduate work, while holding down a teaching assistantship and two part-time jobs.

My parents were supportive, but my in-laws were leery of my vocational choice to continue my education full time due to my growing family responsibilities. My decision to continue professional training was never a lasting question for me as it felt authentic and workable, in spite of the growing family responsibilities.

At the time, it was a choice for me to play it safe by keeping a full-time job at GM that paid reasonably well or risk pursuing full time an advanced degree with uncertainty about success and my vocational future. After discussions and self-examination, I somehow knew my decision would work out in the long term. Looking back, my only vocational question centered on *whether I might have gone to law school if I had applied several months earlier.* More on that matter later.

DAVID T. HELLKAMP

Read, learn, and be inspired to plan.

CHAPTER 02
Early and Middle Adulthood

Early Adulthood. Following successful completion of my master's degree, I applied to several doctoral programs in psychology, including Ohio State University and the University of Ottawa in Canada. I was accepted at both of those programs, but Ottawa required obtaining at least one year of clinical experience in the mental health field before entering the program. I rebelled, but discovered the Ohio State University doctoral program was in temporary shambles in 1964, so I chose Ottawa. Besides, I knew a great deal about Ottawa's clinical program from one of my professors at Xavier who had earned his Ph.D. from Ottawa a few years earlier.

Moving to a foreign country with a different culture with my wife and family was an exciting and very stimulating experience. Although the educational, research, and clinical experiences were arduous, I was being exposed to professors, classes, clinical, and research experiences that I relished in both the English and French cultures of Canada. The family seemed to adapt well also, as the kids were mostly of preschool age.

I remember the winters were longer and harsher than in Cincinnati, but the extreme cold only lasted a couple weeks while the remaining winter was tolerable, like Cincinnati, only consistently below freezing. To our delight, Canada celebrated its Centennial Anniversary while we were there, including hosting the World's Fair in Montreal, Quebec during our last year. We took great advantage of both events as well as the winter activities. Overall, *I began experiencing a strong feeling of success with my vocational goal.*

I graduated in the spring of 1967 (magna cum laude) with my Ph.D. in hand. In retrospect, *success for me included doing the best I could and achieving excellence.* I chose to begin my first job as a joint appointment, both a full-time Assistant Professor of Psychology at Xavier University and a full-time Clinical Staff member of the Psychology Department at Longview State Hospital, a state mental hospital in Cincinnati, Ohio. I ended up taking this customized job in spite of my unofficial pledge before I decided to go to Ottawa that I would not come back to Cincinnati, other than to visit. Remember that Professor at Xavier with the funny name, Dr. Vytautas Bieliauskas? He was Chair of the Department of Psychology at Xavier, and became very persuasive in my decision to return.

As it turned out, it was one of the best decisions of my working life. I grew to love Xavier even though it was not without periodic "hiccups" for me along the way. I was confronted by a former graduate student colleague of mine from the University of Ottawa at a reunion about 12 years after obtaining our degrees. He asked why I remained employed at Xavier. In reflecting on the question, I realized Xavier kept "growing" in quality and scope, so I experienced no desire to leave, even though opportunities occurred. Plenty of other clinical/consulting professional growth opportunities had also developed for me. My private practice, both clinical and organizational consulting, grew rapidly and successfully. My family and I became firmly entrenched in Cincinnati.

Middle Adulthood. On the personal front, I became more and more aware of difficulties my wife and I had remaining fully invested in our personal/marital relationship. In retrospect, there were multiple reasons for the deterioration in our personal relationship. For me, *one definition of success meant being ambitious educationally and professionally as well as family-wise.* Apart from my family identity, my vocational identity continued developing.

On the other hand, my wife was generally content with her high school level of education. Although devoted as a mother, she had many opportunities as the kids grew older to further her education, to develop a foundation for added vocational and educational identity but displayed no consistent interest to do such. It was just not her desire or goal to do such.

These observations are not meant as a criticism, but rather as examples of how our life goals diverged and the gap in our relationship widened as we moved from early to middle adulthood. Many factors led to the eventual marital deterioration and separation. After several unsuccessful attempts to have her also consider entering professional individual and/or marital therapy to possibly salvage the relationship, I sadly realized reconciliation was impossible. I then initiated a divorce, which was finalized within a year, about 20 years after the marriage began.

In the meantime, two of my three brothers also were involved in divorce from their first wives. Not a good batting average for a family of four children, but not so far off from what was happening nationally with first marriages. All in all, 23 more children were part of my other three brothers' clans. In addition, my first wife was one of 11 children. This made for many, many nieces and nephews, not to mention cousins among the kids, considering the extended families. Even though a number grew up in different parts of the country, efforts are still made to this day among many of them to remain close.

Over the past 25 years or so, it has become an annual tradition that family members make a high priority of attending a Siesta Keys, Florida vacation together. Many cousins and others frequently also show up. Although not in Florida, a special Hellkamp family reunion is planned for the late summer of 2019. Consequently, *maintaining close family relationships has become a strong value and measure of family success.*

The next eight years following my divorce had its ups and downs. For example, the first 11 months or so following separation and divorce was very painful on a personal level. Some difficult experiences at the University also occurred as I was teaching in a Catholic university where divorce was not always looked upon favorably. On top of it, my former wife knew many faculty, faculty wives, and administrative personnel. I generally kept quiet about my side of the divorce as I became more socially withdrawn and sad, along with a myriad of mixed feelings. It was a difficult and complex time for me being the "bad guy" by initiating divorce. Only later in life did others become aware of more balanced reasons for the divorce.

On the positive side, I did receive personal support and insight from a very special, loving colleague, two very special aunts on my father's side (Rose Hellkamp and her sister, "Nettie" Hellkamp Young), my older children, some friends and professionally. Apart from previous friends, I also received social support by meeting new people from joining new groups, such as Kiwanis. Developing and maintaining many more social activities, such as in sports, also slowly added passion and direction back into my personal life.

My greatest social and family challenge *became to continue building solid relationships with my kids,* while working on trying to slowly develop a new personal life for myself. With time and effort, untangling in most areas of life occurred.

My work and social involvements did serve a dual purpose of not only allowing me to continue doing what I loved vocationally, but also keeping me distracted from personal turmoil, especially prior to and during the couple years surrounding the marital breakup. During the next six to seven years following divorce, I was involved in several loving relationships that taught me things about women and myself, including feeling more ready to begin moving on with developing a new personal life for myself.

I was fortunate to experience loving relationships of different types, such as with younger women and women, who as it turned out, had very different expectations from my own about raising children. As time went by, I felt increasing pressures that personal decisions had to be made, sometimes very difficult and painful ones. My decision to commit to marriage was ultimately guided from an analysis and understanding of the conditions of the relationships.

Looking back, I believe, for me and maybe for others, *the most difficult areas of life to work out have to do with family, as well as entering and maintaining loving relationships,* and, if necessary, *attending to a grieving process* when leaving a loving relationship.

Certainly, *raising children is the greatest challenge.* I now know I many times worried way too much when I really didn't need to, and probably not enough on a few occasions when I should have! And, yes, I was a licensed expert! When it is with your own kids, it is definitely a different story. Nevertheless, it all worked out reasonably well with both the kids and myself.

I married a woman (Susan Wideman) who was a friend prior to "dating." We shared many similar interests, friends, and hobbies, such as a love of Xavier athletics, especially basketball, and, later, an annual vacation to a time-share condo in Aruba, which we acquired on our honeymoon and only recently sold. Aruba became a "home away from home" for us as well as for a number of family and friends.

Most importantly, she accepted my large family and we both were ambitious. We are now in our 30th year of marriage. From the marriage, I also gained a loving stepdaughter, Paige Wideman, and a sister-in-law, Kathy Wright, among other family and relatives.

Success in my personal life would eventually include growing relationships with family, many new friends, and others. In other words, *developing meaningful relationships* was very important to me, especially due to the complexities of my family situation. *My primary goal was to give my children the necessary opportunities and support to grow in their own right. This goal has also extended to a number of grandchildren.*

Remember my original dual professional passions of law and psychology? Only during my last 20 years of working life did I have the opportunity to attend law school, no longer with a desire to obtain a law degree, but as a special student to be able to take selected law classes that melded with my professional interests, such as being a consulting forensic psychologist.

After being accepted, I took several classes in Criminal Law, Family Law, and I also studied Constitutional Law. It was an unusual experience since I was significantly older than the other students and sometimes older than my professors! *The experience did bring together my two professional passions in a way to permit me to experience how the adversarial (Socratic) methods, using rules such as with evidence, can differ yet merge with different scientific research methodologies for problem-solving, each with the goal of arriving at truth.*

Success in my professional life also involved trying to have an impact on the specialized fields of Clinical and Consulting psychology as well as the profession of psychology generally. I assumed one has a better chance of doing so by gaining leadership roles in professional organizations. Initially, I volunteered on committees and eventually was elected to the top executive roles in many local, state, and national psychological organizations.

Being elected to serve on the Council of Representatives of the American Psychological Association representing Ohio psychologists was the equivalent of serving in Congress in American politics, as the mission of the Council was to set policy and direction for the field of American Psychology. Serving in all these leadership roles allowed me to stay in the forefront of what was happening in the profession, insights that also played out successfully in my practice, teaching, supervision, and research activities.

Looking Back. Other "successes" in my professional life included 20 plus consecutive years of major grants focusing on helping develop a specialized training program for multidisciplinary professionals in treating underserved persons and their families suffering with severe mental disorders (Hellkamp, 1990; 1993a, 1993b, 1996).

I also consulted as a facilitator for strategic planning and executive coaching in various educational, fundraising, law enforcement (Bieliauskas & Hellkamp, 1973), religious, and sports organizations. My private clinical practice also became very large and successful. I will spare you the details of all those vocational activities, while also recognizing that I experienced a few vocational setbacks, which I will spare myself!

Among a variety of awards and honors received, one of the most memorable was Xavier honoring both my wife and myself at the graduation ceremonies in 2012 with the Paul L. O'Connor Leadership Awards. I believe it was the only time both a husband and wife received the awards simultaneously for their long, independent, "outstanding leadership."

In addition to her many outstanding and caring administrative skills, she was described as a pioneer in helping crack the glass ceiling for women in administration at Xavier. I am proud of all her professional accomplishments. *Success became associated with recognized professional achievements.*

I cherish not only having conferred on me upon retirement the title of Professor Emeritus, but the additional title of Xavier Faculty Athletic Representative to the NCAA, Emeritus.

By far, examples of the most cherished "retirement" gifts were an eighth grade written project to my wife and me from one of my grandchildren (DiPuccio, 2018, Appendix A) and a poem written and verbally presented to me on behalf of the doctoral students, orated in my final class in my last semester teaching (Sobieralski, 2011, Appendix B).

Overall, I would hope success at Xavier and elsewhere, would include among other things:

(1) As the Director of the University Clinic, expanding graduate student clinical practicums in the Psychological Services Center and throughout the Cincinnati mental health community; expanding the psychological services provided by the Center to the population of the greater Cincinnati area and beyond, rather than solely within the Xavier community.

(2) When Chair of the Department of Psychology, chairing a university-wide Task Force of senior faculty to study the Feasibility of Doctoral Programs at Xavier since Xavier had no doctoral programs at the time; organizing the Psychology faculty into committees to begin studying and developing curriculum protocols and identifying other necessary doctoral program structures to be developed; began lobbying the major constituents inside and outside the University to begin supporting the idea of a clinical doctoral program; organized a fund drive which raised $10,000 seed money for consultants and other expenses to develop a proposal; and produced the first solid written detailed proposal laying a functional foundation for the development of the later Doctoral Program in Clinical Psychology. When the proposal was later expanded and the doctoral program started by Dr. Michael Nelson, it did become the first doctoral program established at Xavier.

(3) When serving on the Athletic Advisory Board, including as chair (1991-1999), then as the Faculty Athletic Representative for Xavier to the NCAA (1999-2011), to have helped contribute behind the scenes to the growing collective success of Xavier's athletics.

(4) In the classroom and as a supervisor, researcher, and mentor, to have taught and expanded the students' clinical, psychoeducational, and organizational consulting scientific knowledge base, professional skills, and desire to contribute through their own research to the evidence base of human behavior.

(5) Practicing over 50 years as a diagnostician, psychotherapist, and consultant, to have aided the many thousands of patients, clients, and organizations I was given the privilege to serve.

Success became associated with helping others via parenting, teaching, mentoring, practicing clinically and in organizational consulting, and building psychology programs at Xavier and in community organizations.

As my professional life continued advancing, my personal life continued solidifying. During the later stages of professional life, I found myself, along with my wife, who served in many academic administrative positions, the last as an Associate Vice President of Academics at Xavier, beginning to look ahead to the time when we would each be ready to retire. The shift into planning for the retirement stage in later life was becoming a higher priority in our lives, even though we were still in later middle adult life.

PART II

Planning Different Areas Of Life

The whole world was made for us. And what are we doing with it? (Sir Thomas Browne). If we can inspire and lift just one person, much less more, we have made a difference.

The next section of this book will identify different major areas of life that were important to me to examine for retirement planning. You may approach your own journey in a similar way. The chapters will identify planning issues related to Identity Changes, Finances, Socialization, Housing, Health and Wellness, Hobbies, Intellectual Activities, and Spiritual Areas. Along the way, it should be remembered one will likely define and redefine goals more than once due to opportunities and circumstances brought about by change in your current or later life.

As a rough gauge of reference, planning for Finances should ideally begin in one's twenties. Planning for all other areas in life for a successful retirement can be delayed to late middle life, other than to ideally keep records and/or notes.

DAVID T. HELLKAMP

Read, learn, and be inspired to plan.

CHAPTER 03
Identity Changes Entering Late Life

Whatever anchor points a person may use to identify the onset of later life for themselves (age, retirement, the mirror, etc.), I believe one must continue to be reasonably secure about one's personal identity. That, for me, was very different from feeling secure about my work or professional identity. As I approached retirement time, it involved not just stopping or cutting back my professional work activities, but knowing myself well enough to realize I am "more" than my professional or work identity and the status attributed to it.

To do that successfully involved both (1) being comfortable with the change, and (2) planning for the change. From the standpoint of hindsight, I would mention that similar dynamics could also be applicable to earlier major life transitions; for example, deciding as a young man to become a psychologist rather than pursuing some different vocational direction, the GM job or law.

(1) *Feeling Comfortable.* A major part of feeling comfortable with the change in identity and status entering retirement centered on a recognition that both my passion and patience (tolerance) for work conditions and requirements were lessening greatly, while passions for other goals were growing. Specifically, internal changes were occurring as to my level of passion to continue with high energy my professional activities, coupled with a lessening of emotional tolerance for my daily, structured work activities.

This phenomenon was occurring in spite of being involved with professional activities that previously reflected my greatest work passions, such as being able to continue teaching graduate courses, one that I introduced into the curriculum, while also mentoring and collaborating with outstanding students, student-athletes, staff, faculty, coaches, and administrators.

In other words, I was becoming more discontent, sometimes even irritable, with my structured, more routine work activities, while discovering more contentment on a deeper level with giving them up. While all this was happening, I was developing new challenges and goals. All this change started occurring in my mid-sixties, for others, the age varied.

Once I fully retired, I learned it was important to mentally divorce myself from any responsibility for those activities, realizing I was neither indispensable nor any longer in control of those activities. To do such involved recognizing it was now time for others to carry the ball, no matter what that might mean for the continuation of the specific work activities. If one continues allowing oneself to be mentally involved with work activities after giving up control of them, one is likely to experience stress and tensions, especially if things are perceived as not going well.

Some of my friends did not give up total control of their work. This worked out positively for some of them because they were careful in defining their roles and responsibilities. Others neither defined their roles clearly and/or easily gave up control, and they seemed to struggle with their new lives. Contentment associated with those remaining work areas was breached.

This whole process was not merely an intellectual decision, nor something that happened overnight. On a deeper level, it was no longer as important to experience myself primarily as a psychologist, professor, researcher, clinician, consultant, administrator, or "doctor." In its place, I was transitioning my identity to becoming a retired professor and psychologist, a person without structured work commitments and responsibilities, and a person who wished to continue a process for defining and redefining retirement (late life) goals in an age-appropriate and passionate manner.

The shift in identity was significant, very noticeable to me, and most importantly, a "process" rather than an "event." Most of what was happening to me was welcomed. It was no longer necessary or important to impress anyone, not even myself. The change I felt seemed right and earned!

(2) *Planning.* As to planning for the change, I started about 12 years before I fully retired by spending many hours talking to colleagues and selected friends who were either close to retirement or already retired. I also did a very thorough review of the latest literature on retirement. My hope, over time, was to learn as much as I could about what to expect and how to prepare for retirement.

I learned some people worked at full pace till the day they retired, whereas most others began pulling back on their professional or business responsibilities several years before total retirement. I chose to follow the latter path. There was no big surprise when I actually totally retired and, as implied, I felt psychologically ready.

I've noticed some of my peers have struggled with this change in identity by psychologically holding on, or trying to hold on, to their previous work identity. Some were forced into retirement, not having much chance to prepare. Such termination presents different issues within a compressed time.

For the ones who chose to retire, it was as though some did not identify or plan solid goals for where they were heading, but rather seemed to mostly plan for leaving their work lives. In other words, they knew what they were leaving, but were not psychologically ready or reasonably clear as to their goals with regard to their retirement. They expressed having a difficult time setting goals for where they were heading. Other times, they just could not let go of their work identity. Some did not even think much about retiring.

Not too long after retiring, they would report being bored, sometimes depressed. It did not appear to be a good or relaxing time for them. Any contentment experienced was compartmentalized to only certain areas of their lives. In business terms, they did not have a complete or satisfactory exit and/or succession strategy. In spite of all these dynamics, the change to retirement even when successful still had a side to it that included the experience of "loss," the loss of work identity and status.

Transitioning into retirement also involved other new experiences of "loss" for me in a number of different areas of life. I will attend to some of the losses below, including how such changes can add new layers to one's self-identity. As much as possible, one needs to be prepared for such losses.

Success involves continually working to learn about oneself, including one's effective coping skills. All this was extremely helpful as a method for preparing for retirement; that is, to learn how to feel reasonably secure and content.

CHAPTER 04
Finances

Needless to say, one major contributor to feelings of security, success, and contentment was to have acquired a reasonable financial foundation for retirement.

Not being born into wealth, I am grateful to a colleague and former Dean of the Business College (Hailstones, 1969) in my early career at Xavier for giving me the best financial advice about preparing adequately for retirement. I was in my late 20's at the time and he was in his 50's. During shower and dressing times following daily pickup basketball games at noon among faculty, staff, and former college players, we would have "life" talks.

One such topic included sage advice to make sure I maximized contributions to my retirement account at the University, giving it a high priority, even though I was young and retirement saving was not high on my list for how to spend my limited money. *I learned wealth can be obtained in small steps over a lifetime.* Just as important, he also strongly recommended the monies be kept invested in the various stock mutual funds, not annuities, bonds, or money market funds, even though greater variability in value and stress would occasionally occur when market pullbacks would occur. Over the long term, he believed strongly you would maximize your returns. To invest monies from my limited income at that young an age for retirement was sometimes difficult and required sacrifice and self-discipline, sometimes much easier to talk about than carry out.

Additionally, I was advised to always try to have more than one source of income, also setting aside portions of that income in investments and other tax-deferred retirement accounts. As a clinical and consulting psychologist, the advice helped encourage me to continue building a part-time practice. A little later in my life, he and others encouraged me to pursue how to directly invest monies into individual stocks and real estate, both in retirement and personal accounts.

By following such advice, he stated I would put myself in the best position by retirement years to have developed a solid financial foundation. He was right. It worked for me. By accumulating a reasonable financial nest egg over the years, I was in a position to choose when and how I wanted to retire, not to discover whether I would be able to retire.

The transition from work to successful retirement also required dealing with many other financial issues, not just how one has accumulated money. I will not spend time elaborating on them, but mostly, just listing them. They included learning about the details of such things as Social Security policies and payouts, life insurance specifics, how to understand and control taxes, and how best to house and administer your investment and retirement accounts. For today's young persons, learning how to maximize Roth IRA accounts would be one very high priority of retirement planning to master as early as possible.

Very importantly, it was also necessary to develop a will, and, later, when an estate and family responsibilities expanded, a relevant trust. Additionally, developing directions for continued medical treatments when health decisions or death may be imminent. All usually require tweaking every so often due to both changing conditions and the belief on my part that a trust, in particular, can become a successful process for interaction with selected adult family members about your wishes. In that way, one can minimize, if not eliminate, any family conflicts after you are gone.

Later in life, if appropriate, become familiar with specific retirement benefits from your employer and, if necessary, negotiate them. Health insurance plans, including Medicare plans, are critical. Up to our retirement years, both my wife and I were covered by private health insurance plans provided by our employer (Xavier). We considered the private plans extremely good. We had the option to continue with the private plan when we retired.

To our surprise, we discovered Medicare plans were much more comprehensive and significantly less expensive than continuing with the private insurance plans offered by our employer.

We were not in a boat by ourselves. A friend and former CEO of several different major companies before he retired alerted us to the benefits of Medicare. When I researched how Medicare could be better and less costly, I discovered a minimum of 40 cents of our private health insurance dollar at the time was going to other expenses (administrative costs, profits, dividends, etc.) other than to our health care!

With Medicare, at least ninety percent of every dollar spent on insurance would go to health care! That extra thirty percent plus of every dollar going to health care makes a huge difference in health coverage and cost. Our friend, the former CEO, and we chose the same Medicare plan.

I now realize at least one reason why private insurance plans don't want "socialized" medical care to replace and/or regulate them. The private insurance companies and their executives are making huge amounts of money without government competition.

Another goal I prioritized was to minimize operational expenses during retirement years, so as to avoid becoming a slave to debt. Unlike current conventional wisdom, it was also important to me to stay active in investing and not to become too conservative in my choices, just because I was now retired. Unlike with previous generations, there are likely many more years remaining during retirement to support oneself while leaving some financial resources for family members and charities.

Of note, keep in mind tax laws can change and may require restructuring of how your monies are handled. Although I strongly encourage one to become familiar with retirement funds and investments, one should always consult with a financial and tax expert for assurance and/or handling of one's finances. Learning how to use a reliable and valid computerized tax program, Turbo Tax, can also be extremely useful.

Overall, adequate finances (and financial planning) are one major source of feelings of success, security, and contentment, but only one major source. Other areas of life also need to be addressed. The next area is extremely important for success and contentment, dealing with family, friends, and acquaintances.

CHAPTER 05
Socialization Issues

During retirement years, I believe continued relationships with family, friends, colleagues, and in my case, former students, acquaintances, and others are extremely important to underlying feelings of "success" and "contentment" in retirement. Generally, family is most important to me.

Family. As indicated above, my family consists mostly of many caring and compassionate persons. I sometimes joke to others that my family is so large that it is no longer just a family, but a community. Because of the size and blended family complexities, it sometimes took (takes) much effort to deal with even the mere mechanics of communicating with all, much less interacting with each in more meaningful, personal ways. Sometimes it is overwhelming. Other times, it is extremely fulfilling.

Watching and sometimes helping family members develop independence and growth in their own lives is most fulfilling and a source of major pride. I became very proud of all seven kids, from Jeff and Joe, to Jeannette and Julie, to Jamie and Jon, and stepdaughter Paige. I am also proud of my grandchildren (and great-grandchildren) as they age and mature.

For many of us parents, as our kids, spouses, and grandkids grow into adulthood, even with their own families, they too will continue to occasionally experience significant turmoil in their lives. As an example, I am especially reminded of the major trauma my second daughter, Julie, her husband, Nic, their four kids, and basically the entire family, experienced with the sudden, horrendous death of Nic's sister and loss of her husband, leaving two very young children, ages two and four, whom Julie and Nic quickly absorbed as part of their own family, raising them as their own. I, like so many others in the family, are so proud of them, while greatly respecting their strong and generous family values.

I am also very proud of my oldest son, Jeff, his wife, Mary, and their five children. Jeff is an entrepreneur, owning his own small plumbing company as well as being a successful landlord. He and his family are very generous with providing both his professional services and family attention to many in need, even though they encounter occasional pressures.

Jeannette, prior to breast cancer, was a successful corporate business executive. Following medical treatments, she fought to redefine herself successfully as an emerging realtor since she no longer desired large corporate life. She appears to have rediscovered a vocational passion in real estate. I am so proud of how she has become the "Auntie Mame" of the family, pitching in to help anyone in need.

Jamie, with his wife, Jen, have also experienced earlier stressors, but have matured into a very productive businessman, teacher, and loving parents. The youngest, Jon, has settled in as a building contractor, along with raising triplets, a monumental and extremely dedicated task. So proud of all.

My stepdaughter, Paige, has followed my wife and me into university life as an art professor, already publishing her first textbook. So proud of her and of all my children and their families.

I would be remiss if I did not mention one very special former student-athlete, Michael Hawkins, who became an "adopted" member of our family over the years. My son, Jamie, befriended Mike when they both started at Xavier as freshmen. We have all remained friends ever since.

I must note numerous other students and student-athletes without naming them, who also continue to mean so much to me. I hope they have learned something from our educational interactions, as well as success and life. I certainly have learned from them. They are members of my work "family."

During these later years in life, I learned it is important to remember one's children are no longer kids. It is now necessary for them to solve their problems on their own. Even if I am not in total agreement with each of their solutions, I believe it is always important to provide emotional support for them, not rejecting them for their decisions. In other words, it seems always important to remember there is a distinction between emotional support and agreement. It is important to be there for them but typically to offer advice and help only when asked. Waiting for that request for advice or help, whether direct or indirect, is definitely not always easy. Overall, I love my kids and am very proud of their overall values and problem-solving.

When a child has special disability needs and grows into adulthood, it can make a more complicated situation for the parents to resolve. Joe experienced severe learning disabilities throughout his life. It was necessary to monitor areas of his life on occasion. Many difficult decisions had to be discussed and resolved at different times. Nevertheless, Joe demonstrated enormous integrity and persistence in his work and family life. He put family and work responsibilities first in his life. His sons, Sean and Mark, have become very fine men, fathers and/or stepfathers, and wonderful grandchildren.

I can empathize completely with other parents dealing with children with severe disability issues, but can say without reservation, stand with and behind them.

As a side note, I have also learned it is very challenging today to have a large family if your personal goal is to maximize each child's personal growth. Suffice it to say, 60 years ago, very different cultural standards with regard to marital roles and family expectations existed. As one example, it was not uncommon for the married male in my generation to be the provider and work very long hours, while the wife worked at home caring for most family responsibilities. In today's generation, a greater effort is made by each partner to achieve greater balance in family and work responsibilities, along with an effort to balance work and play. I highly value those efforts. It was, and still is, not easy raising a family, even if the family is much smaller. Most retirees stay active with their families.

Many stressors will occur, sometimes testing you to the core. My second oldest son, Joe, was diagnosed with ALS in my first year of retirement. He moved in with Sue and me while the disease progressed rapidly to severely imprison him in his body prior to his passing away the following year.

About the same time, my oldest daughter, Jeannette, developed breast cancer requiring much adjustment as well as serious medical and family attention. Shortly thereafter, Dick, the second oldest of my brothers passed away, having battled cancer for years. It started with skin cancer.

I was then also diagnosed with cancer of a parotid gland and surrounding area. The source of the cancer was considered to be skin cancer, which I have fought throughout middle adulthood and later life. Following surgery, during a period of daily radiation treatments, I experienced my identity expanding to include an outer layer of being a patient.

Overall, it was a horrific period of three plus years for family members and me. On the positive side, I am proud and relieved to say both my daughter, Jeannette, and I are cancer survivors! More recently, another loss occurred as my next oldest brother, Larry, passed away.

Life Lesson. I point out these events as examples of life experiences that were extremely stressful and reflected mostly unanticipated loss, but paradoxically for me, did not destroy my underlying feelings of life contentment. To be sure, significant situational worries, anxieties, fears, and justified "holy" anger, among other feelings, were experienced. Sadness and grief enveloped me for longer periods of time. An inner void has never disappeared, especially surrounding the loss of my son, parents, brothers, and a couple good friends, but has become manageable.

Nevertheless, a soothing, more pervasive inner feeling of contentment remains. Perhaps, how one perceives a stressor is more important to one's coping with it than the severity of it. I do remember thinking during those times I had no direct control over those and other enormous stressors. Maybe that was a coping mechanism that worked for me. Regardless, I now count every day as a blessing!

Although periodic health and other stressors with various family members and myself continue to occur from time to time, underlying contentment tends to remain, in spite of worries and concerns. As always, genuine loving support and compassion from family and friends was (and is) extremely important for all of life's surprises.

Spouse. If married, support from and for your spouse is also very important, continuing during retirement. We did not experience any major adjustment problems entering retirement as we experienced more time together. Prior to and during early retirement, many people freely spoke about their own or other couples' major adjustment problems with each other because of suddenly being together much more than when working. Maybe we were just more prepared because, among other factors, we have many similar interests and have freely given each other individual space to do our own things. In other words, we both felt comfortable with our separate identities. Nevertheless, late-life stage relationship issues still keep us competitive and challenged on occasion!

Friends and Acquaintances. Maintaining selected wholesome friendships and special acquaintances as well as developing new ones during this stage of life is very important, just as it was in earlier periods of life. It is still necessary to take an active role in such endeavors.

For me, I have developed, joined, or maintained several breakfast groups (a ROMEO group: Retired Old Men Eating Out!), discussion groups, retired faculty groups, an Emeritus lunch group, a high school luncheon group, book clubs, political groups, and a neighborhood club, and many Xavier and other special friends.

My wife and I are avid supporters of Xavier University sports, especially basketball, and value those friendships and acquaintances very much. Active efforts to maintain relationships with my University faculty colleagues, staff, and some former students are also very important. Apart from mutual friends, my wife has socially networked in similar ways, especially developing lasting bonds with the multitude and complexities of my side of our blended family.

Pets. One final aspect regarding socialization, not with people, but with pets. As most pet owners have learned, pets can provide a companionship and special relationship with a person at any stage of life. As we get older, pets can help provide for the retiree a shield against loneliness and social isolation. With a little training, pets can also be taught basics for helping persons with certain disabilities, including aging disabilities. For the retiree who has been the more nurturing type of person and is able to care for the pet, the relationship can be very special.

DAVID T. HELLKAMP

Read, learn, and be inspired to plan.

CHAPTER 06
Housing Questions

About 25 years ago, the best man at our wedding and his wife invited Sue and me to stay with them at their newly acquired beachside vacation home in the Outer Banks in Duck, North Carolina. While vacationing, we all discussed issues about our future retirement years. They thought it might be nice if we also would buy a vacation home in the Outer Banks and later all retire there together. Although the idea was enticing, it also became the beginning of many serious discussions between my wife and me as to where and how we wished to live during retirement years.

Housing Issues. Four ideas emerged over time for both of us. (1) We decided to stay in Cincinnati. Most of our families, friends, and hobbies were already established there. (2) We decided to convert our home into a vacation home in addition to our residence, thereby giving our family more relaxing options. (3) We selected a home that would easily convert into living space on one floor if our physical condition would someday require such. The home was also large enough to accommodate family functions. (4) A high priority was given to remaining in our home for as long as we desired and/or could, since we believed that a familiar environment would be soothing during later years.

Senior living or nursing homes were pretty much ruled out, due primarily to what would be a change from an independent lifestyle to more of a communal lifestyle, which we did not desire. Needless to say, each person or couple must prioritize for themselves what they prefer for retirement living.

I believe at some point during this last period of life, serious reflections and discussions about living at home versus nursing homes or elsewhere need to occur among spouses, relevant family members, or selected others. Among other issues, it is important to identify whose needs are really being served when decisions are made.

Such a decision can be very stressful for all involved, if not handled with as much diplomacy and corroborative medical, psychological, and family evidence as possible. For most seniors, the loss of independence, control, and familiarity in areas of one's life are very difficult lifestyle changes and could breach contentment. They would be difficult changes for us. At the same time, the stress and worry for the safety of senior family members can also be extremely vexing for younger family members, if not reasonably resolved.

CHAPTER 07
Health and Wellness

Reaching later stages in life is synonymous with health concerns, even if they are not already present. Longer lasting aches and pains began primarily in my sixties and became more of an issue in my seventies. Minor surgeries along with the diagnosis and treatments for my cancers (thyroid also) occurred. I am becoming more and more aware that we start outliving some of our body parts and organ systems during this stage. The good news is that advancements in dentistry, the behavioral sciences, and medicine can aid us greatly in dealing with a number of these issues.

Preparing the Body. I have been working for years to help prepare my body for the aging process. Such preparation was not by chance. A mentor of mine, that man with a funny name (Bieliauskas, 1981), twenty years my senior, began preaching to me in my mid-forties to keep my body systematically active as long as I can.

From childhood on, I always had interests in competitive sports. As an adult, I played pick-up basketball, baseball, and other games. Those and other sporting activities continued into my fifties. I always gave priority to physical activity. In my sixties, it became more difficult, but I stayed very active in the yard, around the house, and elsewhere.

Since the cancer, I give top priority to systematically working out at the gym three times a week. These workouts, including walking at least a mile, sometimes riding a stationary bike, and 10 to 14 different but age-appropriate weight exercises, have likely made a difference in my energy level, endurance, strength, and physical appearance. For me, these activities sometimes require real effort and work. As a matter of fact, I occasionally tell others the closest I get to "work" these days is "working out."

Being reasonably smart about diet, not smoking, drinking in moderation, and trying to get adequate sleep add to my state of reasonable health. No doubt, good genes and good luck also play a role. Being retired with time to do what I want coupled with reasonable health is a great combination and can't be overstated as an important foundation and source of contentment during this stage of life.

Prior to completing this book, I tore my left knee tendons (quads) in an accident. Surgery was completed within a week of the accident. As a result, I was relatively immobilized for a number of months. During a routine checkup, I was also informed that a pre-existing ascending aortic aneurysm had recently grown close to a concerning size. In addition, calcium buildup was occurring in my artery and veins around the heart. I characterize these incidents as more of my late life's surprises!

The injury took a toll on my exercise habits for almost five months. My blood pressure shot up considerably at the time. I worried about maintaining my cardiac, respiratory, and strength objectives during this rehabilitative and treatment period, especially considering my age. For the first time in my life, I experienced significant physical deterioration as a very real, deeply threatening, and imminent possibility. A sobering reality!

At the same time, I took solace in the fact that I am not the first person to experience such late-life traumas. Therefore, I hoped to find workable solutions from the medical team and strong social and family support, in order to achieve a complete return to my previous physical form. I am happy to report my plan is working!

Point of Emphasis. The moral of this story: stay physically active and use good judgment in an age-appropriate manner. To the young, it may sound somewhat silly, but age-appropriate includes not doing many things that were previously very routine, such as climbing ladders, not walking on steep hillsides, lifting heavy items, continually watching your step against falling, and even recognizing and freely giving up performing simple refined motor activities due to minor asymptomatic hand tremors, such as using a hammer or screwdriver! In other words, allow others to perform such routine activities for you. That is easier said than done, as I found it takes some time and practice to adjust, to learn to ask others for help!

At the same time, I can't ignore many of my friends and acquaintances that have already experienced significant chronic illnesses, deceased or disabled partners or offspring, or other losses in their own physical functioning. Sometimes, remarkable coping skills are displayed, sometimes not. For sure, reasonable health permitting one to be mobile, participating in everyday age-appropriate activities, adds to considerable contentment during retirement.

Sex and Aging. I am also adding a few observations about aging and sex life issues. Sex life is a topic not discussed in many previous writings I have reviewed regarding retirement planning. Although awkward for many to focus on, it should not remain a taboo topic. Paradoxically, in many of the different social groups I meet with, sexual changes and difficulties as a retiree will periodically be brought up as a topic of conversation, but usually in a joking or sarcastic manner, while, in my opinion, with genuine underlying concern and/or frustration.

In my professional life as a psychotherapist and marital therapist, a person's sex life was discussed frequently in a serious manner, not always as a given problem. In a marriage course I co-taught for years, discussions about sexuality were topics of marked interest. Certainly, one can easily find serious scientific and clinically based publications available on the topic, but they are mostly dealing with sexual issues of the young through middle-aged persons/couples. Only more recently are more articles focusing on sex in the aging populations (Stibich, 2019). Unless familiar with such information, my impression is many, if not most, older persons may be left with misinformation, especially about sex and the aging process.

Unlike all other human behaviors, the life cycle of sexual functioning is very different for men and women as aging occurs. In other words, do not expect sexual desires and performance to necessarily be the same for your partner as it may be for yourself. Men, for example, reach their peak of sexual responsiveness and capacity around ages 17 and 18, whereas women do not do the same until their 30's or 40's. Men and women also decline after those peak years at different rates, women generally declining at a slower pace than men.

Yet, there can be wide individual differences in all these changes among men and women and even sometimes within the same person at different times in their life, depending on many conditions. Certainly, such factors as disease, drugs, and alcohol can contribute to marked individual differences.

Separate beds or bedrooms are also not uncommon, due to different physical conditions and sleeping habits.

One critical topic an aging person should address has to do with what sexual expectations one has for themselves, and/or for their partner. Expectations are based on many factors, both physical and emotional. If your expectations remain as they were when younger, frustration and disappointment may follow. We no longer live with young bodies, nor do our bodies react in the same manners as they did when we were young. Consequently, it is necessary to let go of those earlier expectations. It is now time to be more creative in how we live with our sexual expectations.

Moreover, as we get older, the expression of sexual intimacy may need to be redefined for oneself and one's partner. Such a process can include experimentation along with discussions. Ideally, such expectations and intimacies should be discussed and agreed upon. For many successful retirees, one's definition of sexual activity is much broader than when we were younger, but can still be as meaningful and even more fulfilling. If lulls have occurred, it is suggested efforts be made by each party to deal with the situation. If not able to reach an accord, one can consider a consult, talking to a counselor, your family doctor, or find some other trained expert.

As with all other life areas addressed in retirement years, one's sexual life should also be discussed and resolved as considered necessary. It should be known surveys indicate up to 40 to 54 percent of people are sexually active from age 65 to 80. Remember, many persons in this age category have significant disabilities that could hamper sexual experiences, so the stats can be somewhat deceptive.

Maintaining or jumpstarting your sex life should be explored by persons and/or couples throughout aging. Bottom line, one's sexual activities may change, but should not stop without reoccurring discussions and mutual agreement.

Two final points. First, I have primarily focused on persons in relationships of some kind. If without a partner, one does not need to forget one's sexual life, depending on one's health, values, and belief systems. Second, just because we are older, one is not exempt from contracting a sexually transmitted disease. Safe sex should remain a high priority.

CHAPTER 08
The Importance of Hobbies

A true hobby is a form of love. The object of this type of love is an activity rather than a person. Common examples for retirees can include some combination of reading, teaching, writing, playing games, building things, gardening, watching and maybe even playing selected age-appropriate sports, traveling, and movies. Sometimes, bucket lists are developed as well.

Hobbies should focus on both work and play activities. A central component of a meaningful hobby is the experience of passion you have for that hobby. If no passion (excitement) exists for the activity, it is not a hobby, just an activity for passing time. Boredom usually sets in fast.

For me, volunteering, mentoring, and other forms of "giving back" are also very important hobbies. I've volunteered on not-for-profit boards while also giving back financially to charitable groups that I know firsthand do great work for students, medically afflicted, and underserved persons. Such activities give extra meaning and contentment to my life. Time and financial support are important ways of giving back.

Another hobby is investing, although technically, the IRS may consider it more of a job. I don't. Actually, I usually spend little concerted time doing it, but do enjoy reading and learning all I can about those limited investing areas I now know something about. I know it is not truly work for me as, like with most hobbies, time passes without my knowing it!

When I taught neophyte doctoral students about clinical or consulting practices, I would advise and instruct them to also learn firsthand about their finances and how to maintain control over both their own finances and risk tolerance for investing. I believe some methods of successful investing use similar skills that good clinicians employ when they have learned well how to diagnose, do interventions, and apply analytics (statistics). However, that is another story for a different forum.

I will not bore you with some of my other hobbies, such as my life with a home workshop or a John Deere Gator! What is, perhaps, most important for the reader is for you to plan by identifying where your own passions for activities are. After all, if you are currently a student, working, or involved with hobbies, I assume you have given (or are giving) thought as to what courses, work activities, or play activities turn you on! In that way, you are in the planning or implementing stage for your life's work and play.

When you retire from work, you have to spend your newly acquired free time doing something. So, in other words, find where your passions exist, identify them, and go for them. If at all possible, do not allow such a process to occur by chance or by someone else's decision. In those circumstances, one is likely to experience tension requiring further adjustment. In other words, be yourself after you feel you have again found yourself for this stage of life.

CHAPTER 09
Maintaining Intellectual Curiosity

It is wise to participate in intellectual activities in all stages of life. As we get older, it remains even more important. As the saying goes, use it or lose it!

Retirees employ many different ways of continuing intellectual activities. Crossword puzzles, computer games, bridge, chess, watching TV, streaming movies, attending seminars, reading, and writing are certainly examples of possible activities. My recommendation is for every person to find and participate in meaningful and passionate ways of exercising their intellect. What topics have you wanted to study or pursue?

What I have discovered since I retired is that the subject matter of my intellectual curiosities has expanded. The necessity when working to keep up with all the readings and work responsibilities related to my University coursework and committee duties, clinical and consulting practices, research demands and interests, and professional political involvements, all constrained my time to devote to other topics of interest. Now, I have free time to devote in much more depth to those topics, especially "curiosity" topics on more cultural, psychological, social, and political levels.

My current intellectual curiosities are multifaceted, although I will focus on three general topics: (1) understanding different thinking styles in personalities of people; (2) keeping current about what informed visionaries have to say about present forces that are influencing our future; and (3) studying the relationship of intellectual curiosity to entrepreneurial activities.

I will elaborate on each of these three topics, more so on the first two. I selected the first two areas because I believe they can help one understand controversial and very divisive issues that are currently topical in our country and the world. You will be the judge.

Thinking Styles

To set the stage, my interest in different cognitive thinking styles traces back to my Master's thesis, which focused on dogmatism (Rokeach, 1960), a theory that built on the research studying the "authoritarian personality" (Adorno, Frenkel-Brunswik, Levinson, & Sanford, 1950).

The second world war had just ended and authoritarian personality research questions were ripe for how dictators like Hitler were able to influence so many of their own people to support them, with many even carrying out atrocities on their own and other people, such as with the Jewish Holocaust.

Today, the research findings about thinking styles could apply to such personalities as Putin of Russia, Kim Jong Un of North Korea, as well as other authoritarian, dictatorial leaders in our world. A theory like dogmatism would also apply to ordinary citizens in society who score high in authoritarian characteristics (dogmatism) in their cognitive styles of thinking.

Most recently, due to the extreme and rigid polarity and divisiveness that currently exists in our country, especially in our politics, I revisited the theory of dogmatism along with many other more contemporary theories focusing on studying different styles of thinking.

In the USA, like many other countries, more people are as much or more polarized, nationalistic, and divisive in their politics than most any other periods in my adult lifetime. This divisive and polarized zeitgeist appears related to eras of unrest, including an atmosphere of heightened emotional volatility, rigidity, fear, distrust, and cynicism. It has reached such a fever, local and national news media are suggesting ways of avoiding conflicts among family members and friends during holiday get-togethers by avoiding, among other things, open talk about politics!

Dogmatism. Rokeach (1960), in his theory of dogmatism, identified how people organize objective reality in their cognitions as being represented by having certain beliefs which are accepted by the person as true, and other beliefs on the same topic as being false (disbeliefs). How a person has learned to handle the relationship of these belief-disbelief issues to each other in their thinking will determine how open or close-minded they are.

Some beliefs become core or central for them, beliefs they consider factual and true. For example, the earth is round and contains many forms of life. At the same time, other beliefs may be considered false (disbeliefs) by the same person. For example, there are intelligent alien life forms existing elsewhere in our universe. With this example, no problem for many people as the beliefs are reasonably compatible.

Somewhat oversimplified, dogmatism enters the picture when disbeliefs become at odds or contradictory with core beliefs. For example, "my best friend is a great husband and honest businessman" (core belief). Then evidence is presented to you that "he has embezzled thousands of dollars from his company and has a long-standing mistress."

Rokeach would describe a person as open-minded (low dogmatic thinking) if he is able to change his core belief about his friend to fit the evidence, assuming the evidence is verified. But what if he refused to change his core belief about his friend in spite of the evidence to the contrary? Rokeach would describe the person's thinking in that instance as highly dogmatic or closed-minded. Why?

Because the highly dogmatic person would need to work out, consciously or unconsciously, how to reconcile these opposing thoughts within themselves. Highly dogmatic thinking would include holding on to the core belief (my friend is honest and a good husband) while being very rigid and inflexible about changing that core belief. In other words, the evidence to the contrary (disbeliefs) of the core belief needs to be dealt with in some way. For instance, the evidence could be denied or considered fake evidence, or considered a conspiracy by people within the company trying to get rid of him, or the person simply devalues the information in some other way.

By walling off the evidence in their mind, the person could then maintain their core belief. They have compartmentalized the contradictory facts in their thought process. In highly dogmatic thinkers, their core beliefs are stubbornly resistant to change by facts or logical arguments. In other words, they become very closed-minded about how they handle their core beliefs, refusing to accept the facts to the contrary.

Obviously, for any one individual, a person will have many core beliefs and disbeliefs both within and across many different areas of their cognitive reality, such as with religion, sports, politics, race, gender, immigration, in their vocational specialty, or even in fantasies.

Returning to the observation of extreme unrest, polarity, and divisiveness that currently exists in our country, especially related to our politics, I began questioning how different "thinking styles" might play a part in it. My question became… is the greater polarization and divisiveness among people possibly related to tenets in the theory of dogmatism and/or other similar theories, reflecting the differing cognitive styles of thinking and/or other personality characteristics?

One rather simple way in which highly dogmatic thinking (closed-mindedness) is expressed behaviorally is when a person quickly assigns a negative label to the other person when discussions begin on a contested political topic. It is frequently done by using a label such as "liberal," "conservative," "socialist," "elitist," "progressive," "communist," "leftist," "rightist," or any of many other labels.

By doing so, the person doing the labeling appears to see little nuance about the meaning of the label. The label is considered a negative or bad thing. In other words, the labeling is serving some other, defensive purpose in the discussion, a way of devaluing the person, thereby, not dealing with the core beliefs that may be subject to contradiction.

Also occurring, the person, not the particular idea, is what is usually quickly labeled. If confronted about the labeling, let's say, by asking for a recognized defining set of criteria for the label, such a process will frequently trigger agitation, many times with the discussion being diverted from the topic at hand or ended. With such avoidance reactions, one does not need to deal with possible contradictions in their own belief-disbelief thinking.

As a more specific example of the above, the person with a highly dogmatic style of thinking might quickly label a person as a "socialist," when an emotionally laden political topic such as universal health care is brought up. The label will be again be used as a descriptor of the person, not the concept. The highly dogmatic person will find it difficult or impossible to see the person with such a view as merely describing a different method or idea for setting up, regulating, and paying for health insurance. Socialism is overgeneralized as being central to all of the person's politics. "He (she) is a "socialist."

The highly dogmatic style of thinking includes pigeonholing the other person, not merely the idea, as a "socialist." They frequently tend to see the category, socialism, as bad and not a desired American belief, or, if accepted, would definitely lead to extreme or pure socialism, an all-or-nothing and unacceptable situation for them.

The low dogmatic thinking person might experience the concepts of capitalism and socialism in our society as two economic philosophies on a democratic continuum, ways of governing or providing for different types of products/services. For instance, in the USA, we are predominantly a democratic capitalistic economy, even though many services/products are provided, regulated, and sometimes "owned" by the government, by definition, democratic socialism. Examples of such democratic social programs would include our military, police and fire departments, social security system, public education systems, including state universities, roads and highways, the VA hospital system, and most prisons, to name a few.

At the socialistic end of the democratic continuum, such services or products are not governed by the profit motive, but by the principle of equality, that is, the services should be available to all persons in a targeted population.

In a similar way, most older Americans currently tend to believe they have a good form of health insurance known as Medicare, which emphasizes a democratic "socialistic" method for overseeing much regulation of health care, even though it currently also incorporates private insurance companies (democratic capitalism) as the method of delivering and helping pay for the services. Consequently, the person with low dogmatism might think of single-payer or universal health care system as one type of Medicare for all, not something just for seniors.

To the open-minded person, it would not mean America is abandoning capitalism as the predominant economic philosophy. Through such a social system, such products/services could be made available to all that seek them, not merely those who can afford them. In contrast, many other services/products would still be considered better served by a more capitalistic, profit motive system; for example, the type of car you wish to own.

To restate, if one conceptualizes a democratic republic as a continuum with pure capitalism at one end of the continuum and pure socialism at the other end of the continuum, low dogmatic thinkers would assume a large, diverse, complex society, such as ours, is best served when the collective fulcrum is more toward the capitalistic end rather than the socialistic end of the continuum.

It is further reasoned it would not benefit the society if the fulcrum were too close to either extreme of the continuum. A pure socialistic republic tends, among other factors, to inhibit individual creativity and likely overemphasize taxation, while, a pure capitalistic republic could unintentionally unleash greed and selfishness at the expense of possibly attending reasonably to the poor, vulnerable, and marginalized members of society.

An overarching but related social value to be seriously considered and discussed might be that some products and services might be considered a right for all, especially if they relate to health, education, and safety. Sometimes, these services might also be supplemented by the private sector, such as done with private education in addition to public education. In contrast, many other products and services might be better served by a more democratic, capitalistic, private sector part of the economy.

A person with a high dogmatic style of thinking is not inclined to think this through or tends to see most everything should be one way or the other, "capitalistic" or "socialistic," which is a central, core belief for them. They are closed-minded to nuances and complexities of reality if such nuances do not fit with their central, core beliefs.

In the highly dogmatic thinker, their personal beliefs about politics and other forms of cognitive reality are rather fixed and inflexible, thereby devaluing any serious discussion about any possible merits regarding the topic. In politics, such highly dogmatic thinking would account for why many very staunch base supporters of a politician would continue to support them in spite of objective evidence to reconsider the support.

So, persons who quickly label a person rather than the idea as "this or that," have fixed political central beliefs regarding what is true while automatically classifying opposing data as false, even when it is evidenced-based, and do not have recognized criteria to back up the use of the labels, are all behavioral signs of a highly dogmatic, closed-minded style of thinking.

On a collective basis, from a leadership perspective, a high dogmatic style of thinking in a self-centered, manipulative leader can pit one group against another by creating divisiveness through labeling. Such a leadership style emphasizes differences among people rather than sameness. The divisiveness created will be expressed by frequently labeling the other group as "bad," "lazy," "unmotivated," "criminal," or "animalistic," as compared to themselves.

Such a negative association will imply the labeled group is very different from the labelers, in the process devaluing the other group, while wishing to dominate or control the other group in some way, thereby empowering themselves. Such divisiveness can set the stage for distrust and animosity, and ultimately can provide a potential for both individual and mass violence, if people act out their feelings, believing they are either being pushed in a corner or under attack.

Today, among some powerful leaders, man-made climate change issues can provide another good example of differences in dogmatic thinking styles. In the highly dogmatic thinking leader, scientific information about man-made climate change is reduced to the level of false political discussion rather than kept on the level of scientific knowledge. When confronted about such a reductionism, closed-minded thinkers will frequently deny science has anything substantial to say about man-made climate change and/or see the scientific knowledge as "fake or false" originated by some group other than their own, again, some group with whom they usually associate fear, distrust, or opposition.

Paradoxically, many people, individually or in a leadership role, who think in highly dogmatic ways, will tend to deny or manipulate, consciously or unconsciously, any relevant evidence or knowledge that runs contrary to their core beliefs, even if the evidence is based in science, law, philosophy, or politics. They ignore or compartmentalize what the knowledge-based facts might be regarding the topic. Additional motivations might also include self-serving financial gain and/or retaining power by satisfying core beliefs held by their political base.

Dogmatism theory would maintain highly dogmatic thinkers tend to overestimate their expertise in certain areas of knowledge, such as with scientific knowledge regarding man-made climate change while, simultaneously, being highly resistant to the notion they do not have the expertise.

Highly dogmatic persons want their opinions and core beliefs supported, not challenged. "Let's stop talking about this" or "it is fake news" are several frequent responses heard when they are challenged. They may not wish to see any other way to understand things while expressing strongly their opinions and beliefs are correct.

Ordinary highly dogmatic persons yearn to find others, including perceived leaders (heroes), who can appear to understand their frustrations and accept their core beliefs, and somehow magically take them back to a simpler, less diverse and more stable time, prior to the social divisiveness. To fill the void, it is as though they need a "hero they can emotionally identify, idealize, and merge with (emotionally based transferences)," even though they may not understand it that way. They frequently experience the leader as: "finally someone is qualified to lead us... is listening to us," or "finally someone is speaking for us... giving us hope."

Ironically, it may not make any difference whether what they are hearing from the leader (hero) is objectively true or not, a frequent by-product of a highly dogmatic communication model. As long as the message fits their central core belief, it is true as far as they are concerned.

Another example of this distortion is in the area of immigration. Today, many immigrants, especially those black and brown, are being demonized and criminalized (labeled) as though such descriptions are true. The highly dogmatic thinker will accept it as true. They do not fact check the specifics of the descriptions.

On social and political levels, it frequently plays out today in other areas of diversity, creating much anger, confusion, and discomfort with movements like "Black Lives Matter," gender role issues like the "Me Too" movement, and a sexual orientation movement like the "LGBTQ movement," to attitudes in other life areas such as in education, the environment, and government.

All of this is also happening when a growing number of people believe the "American Dream" is dying for them. Many of these persons work very hard and still live struggling to meet their basic bills. They are losing hope. The fact the stock market is setting record highs, or the unemployment rate is at a record low does not translate meaningfully into their lives. Ironically, due to their frustrations, many have been more vulnerable and easily sold false core beliefs of idealized power seekers (leaders) who promise them a lot of remedies. Many have become cynical about any promises, whether true or not.

Highly dogmatic thinkers are frequently vulnerable to accepting and/or advancing "fake news" as long as their personal or central core beliefs are bolstered. They can be intelligent and even formally educated but are frequently factually uninformed. They have not learned or ignore the skills of how to distinguish "facts" from "fake facts," and/or don't appear to care to learn to do so.

Such a distorted culture can elevate ignorance to the level of arrogant ignorance as a norm rather than a negative. Note, ignorance can always be tolerated as it leaves open the possibility for learning, whereas arrogant ignorance involves a refusal to learn, while sternly holding on to one's personal (core) beliefs and opinions, a blatant form of closed-mindedness (high dogmatic thinking).

Overall, such an increase in thinking (highly dogmatic) reflects a cultural tendency, I hope temporary, away from an era of "enlightenment" back toward the "dark ages" where the ultimate "search for truth" can become marginalized, relative, or dismissed.

A greater tendency to listen, view, and/or read news or mass media accounts that support one's own central beliefs or opinions also characterizes these persons. When they do hear different views or opinions, they frequently reject the views by, for instance, referring to it as fake news and/or by labeling. In some cases, the highly dogmatic person may withdraw from continued socialization with persons that have different views from themselves, further isolating themselves from other perspectives. Henceforth, greater rigidity, divisiveness, and polarization occur, but serve to protect their core beliefs.

Fantasy-Industrial Complex. From yet another perspective, Andersen (2017) refers to a growing "fantasy-industrial complex" that has and continues to develop, also filling a void. More specifically, people are spending more time with de-personalized social media (Facebook, Texting, Tweeting, E-mails, etc.) and technological fantasy entertainments (e-gaming, fantasy sports, "reality TV," YouTube, virtual reality, etc.) that can emphasize fantasy over reality, including a blurring of what is fact and fiction. The "fantasy-industrial complex" has developed enormous corporate momentum without significant monitoring as to its overall validity or its actual social impact, value, or influence on thinking styles. As time goes by, it will likely become more regulated for a variety of reasons.

Tribal thinking. More recent extremely relevant research reported by Mercier and Sperber (2017) expands our understanding for some other dynamics in cognitive thinking styles. The research assumes that one basic human evolutionary purpose of thinking is to serve a social or tribal ingroup "confirmation bias."

The theory states that "thinking" can be primarily used to justify and strengthen one's affiliation to one's identified social group (tribe) as a primary way to adapt and survive in life. Since survival depends on most humans affiliating with others, the primary purpose of this basic, but necessary use of thinking is to maintain and strengthen affiliation or an experience of belongingness with another person or social group. In the political realm, identifying is usually to a party, Republican.

This type of "thinking," referred to as "tribal thinking," does not require achieving an intellectual goal of "searching for truth." Rather, it only requires lower level human motivations be satisfied, such as the need for social affiliation, a feeling of belongingness to bolster one's identity, gaining power in numbers, and safety for its members, while aligning one's basic personal or central beliefs to those core beliefs of their group (tribe).

In the political realm, the consequences of negative ads can be an example of this type of tribal thinking. Negative ads usually associate the candidate with negative words, images, and/or sounds while labeling specific negative behaviors, as though such specific behaviors are always central to the individual.

In the most recent presidential election of 2016, Hillary Clinton was strongly associated with the negative phrase "crooked Hillary" with a further tagline, "Lock her up." On the other side, Trump was associated as a "con artist and pathological liar" with the added tag lines you "can't trust him" or "he's mentally unfit for office."

The person who identifies with a particular group or tribe, such as a political party, will automatically accept one of the descriptions without any legitimate verification or fact checking. If pressed for verification, they may say they heard it or read it from a "reputable source." They do not authenticate the "reputable source." The information is frequently passed on to others as though it was true. Within social media, which has no fact-checking, such a communication process can reach large numbers of people quickly and in a repetitive manner.

Tribal thinking and high dogmatic styles of thinking are similar in that both are more primitive forms of thinking styles, as compared to the application of "critical reasoning skills." Yet, it appears tribal thinking can be less complex than what one usually finds in highly dogmatic thinking. In other words, tribal thinking can occur without any dilemma as to having to deal with opposing beliefs at the same time. In the case of basic tribal thinking, truth is not an objective, but affiliation. In highly dogmatic thinking, the addition of tribal thinking could account for why the core beliefs become even more resistant to change.

The low dogmatic thinking person will seek legitimate verification before accepting as true any information, such as in negative ads. The more open-minded person will actively seek the documented facts (truth) about any assertions as to the primary motivation, not merely what some in-group says, whether they identify with the group (tribe) or not. Most importantly, any new documented evidence can change their personal or central beliefs on a topic, even if it deviates from the groups (tribes) core beliefs.

In our American society, I would propose there are at least four other common "tribal" in-group categories other than the "political" category that people frequently identify in one way or another. They include (1) religious tribal groups, (2) sports tribal groups, (3) work tribal groups, and (4) ethnic (family, gender, racial, geographical, etc.) tribal groups.

As with the political tribal group, thinking styles in such tribal identity in-groups can be primarily influenced by affiliation, not by truth based on intellectual rigor, due to the fact that within each category, people usually identify and affiliate with a particular tribal group or subgroup because their personal beliefs and emotional attachments are similar.

For example, in the ethnic realm, one usually identifies with a particular gender, race, etc.; in the religious group, one identifies as a Christian, Jew, Muslim, or atheist or some other sect or sub-sect; in the sports arena, it is usually my high school, college, or professional team, and so on. In other words, one frequently experiences a built-in bias or prejudice which can primarily and strongly influence one's "thinking" process in a tribal manner. The stronger the identification for the individual, the more difficult it would be for them to allow someone to challenge their opinions, a likely example of being also closed-mindedness on the specific topic.

The more a democratic culture relies on highly dogmatic and/or tribal thinking styles for its members, the more likely cultish or extremist groups will be found to flourish. In other words, the belief systems of people can be more easily controlled and manipulated. Truth and honesty can also be hidden and manipulated. Leadership is more likely to be at odds with democratic principles. Leadership will likely be authoritarian.

Critical reasoning skills. Persons can be explicitly taught how to transcend basic tribal and high dogmatic thinking styles by employing the intricacies of critical reasoning skills. Philosophers, historians, mathematicians, scientists, legal experts, investigative journalists, and firmly educated others are examples.

However, more and more people are failing to use "critical reasoning" skills as a tool to search for evidence-based "truths" that transcend basic tribal in-group thinking. There are many reasons for the lack of applied critical reasoning skills. Basically, it is just easier not to apply such skills. In its stead, such persons are being influenced to a greater degree than before by fake opinions and alternative facts (storytelling) expressed in repetitive mass communications using basic principles of Pavlovian and Skinnerian conditioning, that de-emphasizes, de-values, or ignores the use of factual critical reasoning in the search for truth and honesty. In its place is repetitive association.

Another complicating factor regarding the decreased use of "critical thinking skills" relates to the use of negative labels that are associated with it. Today, more and more so, people who present facts based on critical reasoning skills are assigned various negative labels such as "elitist," "superior," "liberal," "left wing," or something other. In that way, both the person and the facts are de-valued, allowing the person who does the labeling to maintain their central core belief without experiencing any dissonance with facts that may be contrary to their core belief.

The human paradox is both tribal and critical reasoning skills can serve a necessary, adaptive purpose for every person. Clearly, each form of thinking needs to be understood as to what purpose each serves for human evolution, opinions, and facts (truth).

When facts are unavailable, tribal and highly dogmatic thinkers will be especially susceptible to accept the opinions of "leaders" at face value, a form of authoritarianism. In such instances, the reliance on such information can be based on human hearsay and/or storytelling, which derive from legends, dogmas, and mythologies that are "learned" and passed to others over time. A strong factor underlying the acceptance of an "authority's" word is such persons have a difficult time dealing with ambiguity on a topic. In other words, there is a built-in evolutionary pressure in our cognitions to want an explanation for events rather than being left with no explanation or ambiguity.

Critical reasoning (thinking) skills are based on data, evidence-based information, not hearsay storytelling, and required for open-minded and effective problem-solving. People learn to tolerate ambiguity until evidenced-based facts are found. In other words, they do not jump to conclusions. Teaching critical thinking skills is one of the expressed major goals sought in education, including higher education, regardless of the particular school or the major a student selects.

Compared to tribal or highly dogmatic forms of thinking, critical reasoning requires active and disciplined mental skills (psychological energy and work) in following and applying rules of logic (syllogistic reasoning), utilizing reliable and valid procedures for collecting evidence (knowledge of scientific methodologies, or in law, employing the legal rules of evidence; etc.), and then, substantial corroboration of all such evidence, whether directly obtained or through an established valid and reliable source, not just an announcement on Facebook, a bot, or tweet. At a specialized level, learning critical thinking skills might require numerous courses of study and mentoring in a variety of different vocational fields of study.

In contrast, it takes virtually no psychological effort or mental energy or skills to rely on tribal or highly dogmatic thinking styles to form beliefs and opinions, under the guise of being facts. Our hidden brain (older brain) is wired to automatically draw conclusions or overgeneralize our thinking when events happen, especially when they occur close in time to each other or are posited to be true in some tribal, talking point communication.

As Thomas Jefferson, the primary author of The Declaration of Independence, strongly believed, education, based on the pursuit of (critical) reason, can lead to a political climate that enables the discovery of factual knowledge, which, in turn, can lead to greater experiences of both individual and collective freedom. Such education can also lead to advancements in society via the establishment of a knowledge base such as in philosophy, science, business, law, mathematics, and the arts (Cunningham, 1987). In turn, such advancements can lay the foundation for a strong society (republic), which today, America likes to ideally describe as a democratic republic.

From an evolutionary standpoint, the majority of human beings likely relied on tribal thinking to adapt and survive for at least the majority of past millennia due to the fact most people were not educated and subject to authoritarian leaders. Our American form of government is truly an experiment, putting the power in the hands of the people rather than authoritarian leaders. The "people" must be encouraged to become educated, to learn to think critically.

A more recent treatise titled "The Hidden Brain" also elaborated about the origins of such forms of evolutionary behaviors that drove and still drive such primitive thinking (Vedantam, 2010).

The earliest bicameral man likely experienced nothing more than adaptive behavioral conditioned habits for survival, lacking consciousness as well as any tribal or critical reasoning thinking as we know it today (Jaynes, 1982).

I believe many people today do have an underlying need to eventually know and seek honesty, truth, and knowledge, but in our current culture of unrest, such desires are many times being suppressed, primarily by power-seekers who emphasize primarily tribal goals, especially power, money, and divisiveness over other social groups for self-serving purposes.

Popular contemporary writers such as Andersen (2017), Foer (2017), Hayes (2012; 2017), Maddow (2019), Stoll (2017), Traister (2016; 2018), Vance (2016), and Williams (2017) offer a good sampling and detailing of many more insights for accounting for many changing behaviors and thinking styles occurring in our contemporary culture. I would strongly recommend reading all of these viewpoints. They include a closer look at how many of today's women are viewing gender inequality, gender roles, marriage, and singlehood; how changes are occurring within norms for the white working class; how limitations, possibilities, and stereotypes exist in some corporations, the rural Appalachian subpopulation, blacks, the so-called "elitists" groups, and immigration groups.

As a historical note, very similar distinctions in how human beings think were identified over 100 years ago by psychologist John Dewey (1910) in his classic book, *How We Think*. Although he used different words to describe the different thinking styles, for example ("empirical thinking" vs. "scientific thinking"), he also pointed out many similar descriptions of the different styles of thinking, including ways of teaching higher forms of thinking, what we call today, critical thinking styles.

My purpose in referencing Dewey's work from 1910 is to point out that different thinking styles have been observed, identified, and promoted in behavioral science over many generations in human behavior.

Although different words have been used to describe the thinking styles, the dynamics related to thinking styles have remained fairly constant. Similarly, the specific contents of people's beliefs that are of societal interest at any particular moment in history may change, but not how different thinking styles may be used to understand them, use them, even manipulate them, but more importantly, how to develop them.

Please note, it is not my intent to persuade the reader to any particular policy, political or otherwise. My purpose is to show how the different styles of thinking can be applied to different policies or other reasoned agendas of any type that are contemporary, especially some of the more affect-laden political examples. I believe the different styles of thinking can contribute to our understanding of today's divisiveness, turmoil, and unrest. The ideal interaction of persons with different ideologies would be for each to use evidence-based facts based on critical thinking styles to reach consensus on how to solve differences in opinions. A dramatic and powerful example of this process was demonstrated in a very recent movie: *The Two Popes*.

In that movie, Pope Benedict, who maintained a very conservative agenda in many areas of church dogma, confesses to Cardinal Francis, who maintains a more liberal agenda of church dogma, that the Church needs a pope to lead the church who is connected to the "people of the church." Pope Benedict, who confessed he was not connected to the people while perceiving Francis to be connected, then conveys he will resign as pope and support Francis to become pope in spite of their ideological differences. Such an incorporation of facts based on critical reasoning to solve problems in the church was very touching and difficult, but displayed a problem-solving methodology that leads to success in problem solving based on evidence-based facts, not defensiveness or self-centered power plays. In other words, both men put what might be in the best interest of the church above their personal tribal agendas.

In current U.S. politics, it is currently rare for leaders of one party to transcend tribal forms of thinking, arriving at a consensus for what may be in the best interest of the country (people) rather than what is in the interest of a particular party or leader.

I do believe greater success and contentment can be achieved with the advancement of knowledge, including how the different styles of thinking can influence how knowledge is used in decision-making.

Achieving critical reasoning skills requires strong and effective improvements in many of our current educational systems. There are no short-term answers other than bolstering our educational systems in the value and application of critical thinking skills for more and more of our citizens, ideally a very democratic goal. Any efforts to sabotage education should be identified and confronted. Only authoritarian leaders would sometimes prefer many people not be too versed in critical thinking skills, so as to better maintain control over them.

Finally, the ultimate solution is for people with different perspectives to come together to discuss differences on an ongoing basis, while agreeing on accepted methods to seek evidenced-based facts from false opinions. In that way, they would be in a better position to arrive at a consensus. Not all people will be able or willing to do so initially. That is OK. One should consider this solution as having both short and long- term objectives for reaching more and more persons.

Informed Visionaries

My second area of intellectual curiosity focuses on what informed and erudite visionaries as early as our founding fathers to more contemporary visionaries (Bloom, 1987; Toffler, 1971, 1981, 1990; Gore, 2013; Friedman, 2016) have written about trends influencing possible change, not only in our present lives, but, especially looking to the future. In other words, my curiosity focuses not only on how things appear to be in the present as compared to the past, but also how things might be changing for generations in the foreseeable future.

My intellectual curiosity is primarily present-to-future oriented, whereas those who have little curiosity/vision appear primarily present-to-past oriented. I do believe the past is important for many other reasons (for example, an understanding of uses of power, human patterns, and other general knowledge of people, places, and times, etc.) but it is not as good a trigger today for stimulating my curiosity for looking from the present to the future.

At least three major forces are identified as responsible for accelerating the pace of change we are experiencing in today's world. Friedman (2016) speaks of (1) the fast pace of change in technology (Moore's Law), (2) globalization (markets; cultural and social diversity), and (3) the environment (Mother Nature, including man-made climate changes) in today's world. He observed these three kinds of change as occurring with exponential speed compared to the past. He further believes the speed of change is beyond what could be comprehended in the past.

A cliché such as, "the only thing new in the world is the history you do not know," is considered outdated, particularly when applied to the pace of change. In contrast, the following statement appears much more apropos: "There is no prior period of change that remotely resembles what humanity is about to experience" (Gore, 2013, p xv).

The rate of change may make it more difficult for more individuals to keep up and adapt, what Toffler (1971) referred to as "future shock." The understanding of many societal structures, such as patent laws, educational practices, work conditions, conditions of marriage, energy transformations, how transportation might be conducted, religious rituals, etc., may uproot (migrations) and bring change for people, requiring different attitudes, definitions, policies, and even legislation in order to accept and adapt.

(1) *Technology.* As common contemporary examples of difficulties keeping up with the accelerated changes in everyday technologies, it is not unusual to hear complaints from my fellow retirees about not knowing how to fully use or understand one's latest smartphones, computers, robotics, streaming TVs, artificial intelligence, transformations in energy sources such as electric cars, solar panels, or wind turbines, or to fully comprehend and accept the notion of driverless cars, which may eventually do away with car ownership for many people as a desired way for transportation.

In the near future, even more changes are predicted to occur, making it even more difficult to keep up. Friedman (2016) conjectures, somewhat pessimistically, the acceleration of change in technology will soon surpass most people's ability to adapt. If so, innovations and continuing education within the social sciences, especially human engineering, computer engineering, computer science, law, and STEM research overall, with applications and regulations, will likely be needed to help solve what might become monumental adaptability issues.

I am a bit more optimistic about the future. I believe most younger persons might more quickly adapt to the rapid changes that are occurring than my generation was able to do. They will do this by extending their human cognitive capabilities via, perhaps, budding creative artificial intelligence technologies, or what is being referred to as augmented reality and coding.

In other words, just as our visual sensory capabilities have been extended over the past several generations via the development of technologies that allow us to "see" much more with the naked eye via X-rays, microscopes, telescopes, live TV, and in numerous other ways, they might develop apps that make it "easier" for them to adapt to more complex cognitive issues. On a simple cognitive level involving information and memory, we can now google or ask Alexa for any information we can't remember or have never learned and get it almost instantaneously. Many in my generation are beginning to accept these changes, but, for the most part, are still leery about these changes.

Of equal importance is the need to untangle the relationship between advancing communication technologies and balancing socialization skills, since technologies tend to emphasize individual activity rather than face-to-face socialization, as we have known it.

Learning the skills to be able to distinguish what is fact from fiction ("alternative facts"; "fake news") will also become even more important as communication technologies continue to become more varied, widespread, instantaneous, and, for now, less monitored.

In my opinion, the development of various forms of monitoring should be seriously examined, such as, but not limited to, developing ethical guidelines, which might first identify acceptable values and basic principles in various areas of mass communications. Then, perhaps, using some form of coding and computerized algorithms to help instantaneously organize and analyze relevant, large databases, one might spell out specific ethical principles to help identify the reliability and validity of information communicated.

Mass communications, such as Tweets, E-mails, Facebook, etc. might then be monitored within the guidelines so as to identify what might be fact from fiction. Such guidelines could help to identify misinformation (fake news), which might be produced out of intention, omission of context, or ignorance. Foer (2017) discussed all these issues and the necessity of regulations in more detail.

If schools teach skills and society prioritizes the capacity to distinguish fact from fiction, a greater proportion of the population might be in a better position to use "critical reasoning skills" for distinguishing truths from fantasy. By applying methods that help discriminate facts from fake facts, one would minimize a vulnerability to false news, propaganda, and, hopefully, close the gap in segmented communication patterns, that is, people tending to communicate only with persons who have the same central beliefs or opinions.

Even though I have limited my discussion of monitoring to the area of fact from fiction, it should be pointed out that similar algorithmic methods of monitoring and coding might also be applied to other undesirable social behaviors occurring in mass communications such as bullying, child porn, unwanted sexting, sexual harassment, stalking, fraud, and identity theft. After all, monitoring techniques have already been developed to help various businesses collate a multitude of behaviors about individual consumer buying and other behaviors. These are forms of monitoring.

Of course, staying ahead of hackers will also be a high priority. Similarly, a balance between privacy and the common good needs to be continually examined and maintained. In my opinion, not to monitor in mass communications may leave a person more vulnerable to severe privacy breaches than having reasonable monitoring systems in place for augmenting the reliability and validity of the content.

One example of how some of this can occur is found in the work of Bartlett (2017). Bartlett published a brief description of the problems outlined above with regard to "fake news." He offers his own solutions along with a very valuable listing of suggested existing resources that a citizen could research to decide what may be fact from mere opinion. Whatever the type of monitoring, the ideal way of accomplishing it would appear to me to be a process of collaboration between the public, private, and not-for-profit sectors.

In the process, freedom of speech must continue to be prioritized. Because of the major transitions occurring in mass communication technologies as compared to more traditional person-to-person communications, perhaps subjective opinions in mass communications should not be allowed to override data-based facts. In greater detail, school curriculum along with relevant apps need to better educate as to the distinctions among "opinions," "facts," "beliefs," "valid and reliable evidence," and the relationship "feelings" can have to each.

Without such clarity, one can easily conclude any opinion or belief one feels strongly about must be true, a potentially very misleading and distorting state of "reality" (Andersen, 2017). In contrast, facts that are based on reliable and valid evidence, regardless of the level of feelings, are to be emphasized, pursued, and expressed. As stated by a great former U.S. Senator, Patrick Moynihan, people always have a right to their own opinions, but not a right to their own "facts."

Along such a path, considerable understanding and trust in the "American System" of government may also need to be learned, or relearned and emphasized, particularly among Americans who have been found in recent surveys to be very poorly informed about many fundamental aspects of our system of government (Strauss, 2016). Appropriate civics classes might again become mandatory in all our secondary education.

Our democratic form of government, emphasizing primarily a two-party system, based on laws, housed in an independent executive, congressional, and judicial branch, with their built-in potential corrections, including a free press, all based on a Constitution, Bill of Rights, and Declaration of Independence, is still one of the best structural forms of dynamic government to enable freedom, capitalism, and creativity to flourish, even though still not perfect in its implementation.

If you do not believe it or are unsure, but have the opportunity, visit a country that does not allow freedom of speech, or punishes behaviors not in agreement with their leaders. You quickly learn the strengths of our country, in spite of its problems. I had that direct opportunity in my role as an organizational consultant in Lithuania over a seven-year period, beginning in 1993, several years after the Baltic States gained their freedom from the totalitarian Soviet Union in 1990.

What is perhaps most threatening to our form of government is when leaders, corporations, or foreign governments attempt to condition people to distort its tenets. They create cynicism and distrust about the independence and/or functioning of our branches of government, while questioning the freedom of the traditional news media (free press), many times concluding the free press is spreading false news and discounting truth and honesty.

Such corruptions can be directed by leaders and/or specific individuals or groups of individuals of countries and/or corporations that use money and/or "data systems" ("fake AI distorted messaging") to create similar or other mechanisms that lead to a devaluing, distortion, distrust, and/or cynicism about our system of government or political elections.

From a group dynamic perspective, I would hope the current increased loss of trust in our two-party system, the divisiveness in Congress, the growing concern about the integrity of our presidential leadership, and how the government is "broken," will be solved by our nation working within our system of government.

I believe it is important that private sector "corporate style" dynamics be clearly separated from "government style" dynamics, just as it is important that "government style" dynamics be clearly separated from "religious style" dynamics. The governing of most corporations is usually based on a different leadership style (authoritarian) and mission (usually making money) from that of government's leadership style (democratic) and mission (protection and representation of its peoples).

From a group dynamics standpoint, corporations are usually not run as a democracy, whereas the foundation of our government was set up to allow a democratic republic to emerge. The group dynamics of each are becoming more blurred rather than remaining distinct and complementary. It is not uncommon to hear people say the government should be run like a corporation! If so, our democratic society could eventually be transformed into a very different form of government.

Foer's work (2017) is an eye-opening treatise about how major technology companies are already creating invasive "portraits of our psyches" from the massive databases on anyone using the internet. Such profiles allow these "companies to predict our purchasing behavior and identify many of our wants." If any or all these intrusions happen without reasonable regulation, while directly attacking our democratic beliefs and our laws, our system of government could be changed from one of a republic to one of a dictatorship and/or a fascist state, an alliance of corporations and/or wealth with government rather than an alliance of government with the people (Posey, 1960).

Increased stress about such changes and power shifts is currently being demonstrated in a 2017 national survey, including a sampling of members of both parties (APA, 2017). I hope such sources of large information databases that could condition our beliefs to distort our democratic ways will be appropriately monitored and regulated in the near future.

(2). *Globalization.* Returning to the notion of the fast pace in globalization as anticipated by Friedman (2016) and other visionaries, the generations following mine will probably become much more desensitized to the enormous and quick changes in, at least, both technologies and globalization, considering they won't have known anything different in their lives. Consequently, for them, it may be experienced as "normal." Only current older generations like mine will have lived through the enormous changes in pace of technology, globalization, and the environment during one's lifetime.

It may turn out the speed of change for younger people may not be as important as the creativity involved in being able to develop and monitor stabilizing, user-friendly applications (apps) for augmenting and coding the quick pace of change. An exception may be with the fast pace of changes in the environment. Although our current political leadership is straying from globalization much more so than previous political leaderships, from a group dynamic perspective, it would be foolish for governments to maintain a more nationalistic policy.

For the world to survive, reasonable efforts at developing stable globalization affiliations must be encouraged just as on a micro-level, members of a family (or community) must get along and interact reasonably well to survive.

(3). *Environmental.* "Man-made climate changes" are currently very worrisome due to the very fast pace in climate changes occurring as a result of carbons being released from man-made creations. Although climate change has been occurring for millennia, it has never occurred with such a quick pace as being scientifically documented in current times. Such fast changes could lead to a tragic outcome for humanity in the foreseeable future if no significant resolution is made from this point in time forward (Wallace-Wells, 2017).

I strongly recommend to those who question the validity of man-made climate change to read Wallace-Wells article as a start. The article provides a journalistic summary of many scientific findings addressing numerous potential consequences to human life if man-made environmental changes are not addressed, admittedly highlighting a worse-case scenario. Although the article has been criticized for including some questionable scientific facts, "...the overall thrust of the article is not wrong, wildly misleading, or out of bounds of the discussion we should be having about (man-made) climate change" (David Archer, University of Chicago). Tragically, our US political executive leadership is totally ignorant of these scientific facts, or worse yet, just don't care due to short-term money opportunities by continuing to support fossil fuels.

Unlike doomsayers, I do not underestimate the power of human creativity to solve these problems, even during times, such as now, when one sometimes wonders whether rationality, as opposed to power seeking, will survive.

Entrepreneurial Vision

My third and final intellectual curiosity focuses on how entrepreneurial endeavors correlate with intellectual vision. Entrepreneurial activity can be considered the applied side of vision and curiosity. It involves thinking creatively, many times, thinking outside the box or without a box, while taking the ideas and implementing them. Just as important, it involves learning to take informed risks, sometimes major informed risk to move forward and develop your visionary ideas and business plan (Robb O'Hara, 2017).

Entrepreneurial exploration can entail not just looking for an already established job opening, but learning to evaluate market needs or voids and creating a "job" for you. Such custom job creation for yourself may become "a second source" of income over and above another more established job you may already have. As a retiree, identifying an investing option as a self-directed investor has provided additional income for me, likely my final entrepreneurial activity.

Apart from some of the informed visionaries mentioned above who have published their ideas, I have selected a sampling of other very successful contemporary American entrepreneurial visionaries who have not written extensively but are known primarily for what they have been instrumental in "creating." They include visionaries such as Jeff Bezos (Amazon), Bill Gates (Microsoft), Steve Jobs (Apple), Elon Musk (SolarCity, SpaceX, Tesla), Mark Zuckerman (Facebook), Larry Page and Sergey Brin (Google), and Warren Buffett (stocks and investing).

Conclusion. Needless to say, readers will need to determine their own intellectual areas of curiosity and passion for themselves and how it might play out in their retirement. I would hope more and more of the world's population can be influenced to become more excited about change rather than feeling overwhelmed, angered, or fearing it. The ultimate goal would be for persons to learn to adapt positively to it, no matter what directions it may lead them in life. Identify your intellectual passions and develop them during retirement.

CHAPTER 10
Spirituality Issues

Spirituality includes dealing directly with your values, interests, and priorities. Values and interests help define your character, choices in life work, relationships, and hobbies. Values and interests also help set the foundation for personal integrity, integration, and dircction in one's life via moral character, planning, and goal setting (Sweeney and Fry, 2012).

I have always found it valuable to periodically reflect on how my life is going, in other words, to appraise my values, set goals, and make plans to achieve the goals. Achieving your goals can become a definition of success for oneself. Others may use meditation, retreats, praying, psychotherapy, drugs, hypnosis, mindfulness methods, or something else as a helpful ancillary mode to aid in arriving at similar goal settings and success.

On occasion, either minor or major shifts were made in my life choices. At those times, I hoped such changes would also be in the best long-term interests of any other person involved in the process, knowing in the short term, stress, sometimes intense stress, might occur. Such transitions can be sometimes easy, sometimes very difficult and risky. In the latter instance, they might involve changing vocations and/or changing marital status. For me, on occasion, stress periods dealing with both vocational and personal issues occurred, fortunately, not simultaneously.

One major example in my vocational career, I recognized an opportunity to develop a large, multi-state psychological practice, hiring many psychologists to provide clinical services. Such an enterprise would have enabled me to build a company, very likely providing the opportunity to become very wealthy. I worked up a business plan and found myself perplexed and excited at the same time. After discussions with select others and self-examination, I realized my passions were much stronger to continue doing the variety of academic and professional activities at Xavier and elsewhere, rather than spending my time running a large professional practice, once developed. To my surprise, I also realized becoming very wealthy was really not that important to me. The academic atmosphere and all it entailed was much more enticing. Although I would have enjoyed building the business, I knew myself well enough to know I would not have felt fulfilled running it. It just was not me, but for some others to do.

On a personal level, as discussed above, marital and family breakdown (divorce) was an extremely painful and stressful time in my life. Remnants related to trust issues within certain personal relationships can still sometimes surface to this day, in spite of very loving relationships since.

Ideally, I would not recommend anyone marry and/or have a family today until each partner has developed an identity beyond the relationship itself and has also developed a solid personal and vocational identity. The fact that younger people are marrying much later than the average age of my generation can provide more time for not only their personal but vocational identities to develop. Marriage at a young age is generally highly related to divorce. It certainly was for us.

On a deeper level, spirituality can also involve dealing with one's relationship to God and to organized religions. For maybe the first 70 years of life, I always felt comfortable as a believer. My belief in a Higher Being was challenged when I learned about data-based evidence supporting the Big Bang Theory and Theory of Singularity. Intense reading and rereading of Stephen Hawking's (1996) book, *A Brief History of Time*, along with other work by Hawking (2009) and others (Ferguson, 2012), shook some of my beliefs.

Although aware of many popular philosophical, psychological, and theological arguments (Freud, 1939; Stern and Marino, 1970; Küng, 1979; Jaynes, 1982; Collins, 2006; Meissner, 2001; Kelly, 2012) both in support of or against being a believer, the most powerful evidence for me up till that time was the immense feelings of awe I would experience when I took time out to look up at the sky on a clear dark evening. I saw the stars, reflected on the vastness of the universe, and concluded there must be a Higher Being to account for the existence of everything. Sound familiar, looking to the sky on a clear dark evening? Thanks, Dad!

I am currently working to better understand my beliefs. It has become a late-life spiritual concern for me. For someone like me who looks for evidence before accepting a truth, it appears the acceptance of faith and revelation becomes the primary bases for believing in God. So, spiritual exploration for me is continuing through further study and discourse.

Prior to and following a recent trip to Spain, Manresa especially, I have again become focused on studying the life of Ignatius of Loyola, the founder of the Jesuit Order (Meissner, 1992). This line of inquiry has become of interest to me as a possible avenue for attempting to gain greater spiritual insights from his remarkable transformation in identity from more worldly goals to that of an extraordinary spiritual mission.

From my studies, it became apparent Ignatius was a very complicated personality who opened himself to numerous psychological interpretations, especially during his period of extreme transformation in life goals while living in Manresa. Ignatius defined what are known as the spiritual exercises as a way to gain insight into one's spiritual life.

What I did learn from Ignatius' insights coupled with past discussions with compassionate Jesuits, all left me with my belief that success and contentment are highly related to being "a man or woman for others," a central Jesuit value to be lived. This goal is important to me and does not stop in retirement.

For sure, a desire for some form of immortality is real to me. Perhaps, at a minimum, it is best demonstrated as a vicarious by-product of this book to "live on" when someone in the future reads it and thereby learns something about me as a person and/or relative from the past. The desire for immortality appears to be a primal motive in the life of we humans, maybe nothing more than an aspect of our primary narcissism. The critical question is whether immortality should be reduced solely to a psychological level? Currently, I do not believe it can be that simple.

As to the fact that spirituality in our life can also relate to our relationship with organized religion, I find myself experiencing some conflicting beliefs. I was born, raised, and instructed in Roman Catholicism. I have also become acquainted with various tenets of some other major religions, such as some other Christian faiths, Jewish, and Muslim religions. I believe strongly the majority of the religions can offer hope for the future to their members with a belief in God. Consolation and encouragement can also be provided by being members of their religious group. I also have great respect for many other aspects of organized religions.

But, with a number of religions, I find myself having a couple very serious objections, especially to several major discriminations that some organized religions promote. I will point out in my own religion, Roman Catholicism, the discrimination that occurs against women by preventing them equal status to men in the organization.

Historically, the status of women is either elevated as being placed on a pedestal (Virgin Mary) or devalued by not being accorded equality in status to men. For example, women can't be priests. Such discrimination is archaic and based on tradition and highly dogmatic beliefs that are man-made. One needs to step back from the Catholic culture to really see how archaic and discriminatory the practice is. It still reflects the gender inequalities at the time of Christ as though this status should not or can't change.

Another discrimination I shall mention is the archaic rule that priests should not be able to marry. I believe my religion needs to continue serious discussions to find resolution regarding some archaic beliefs about gender, sex, marriage, and sexual orientation.

I would hope the church continues evolving and maturing to deal with all such issues rather than just discarding them and those who object as being anti-Catholic or with some other negative label(s). By resolving the issues, I believe it will solve many practical problems my Church currently experiences, especially highlighted in more developed countries.

Do you self-reflect about your own spiritual beliefs or issues? Or reflect on your values and goals? I would encourage one to do so periodically in order to achieve success and contentment in one's life. Needless to say, such issues do not just disappear for me as a retiree.

PART III

Final Reflections On Success, Contentment, And Retirement

*May we never envy those that are successful and content, but strive to learn from them.
May our own life journey and retirement then become successful and content.*

DAVID T. HELLKAMP

Read, learn, and be inspired to plan.

CHAPTER 11
Success vs. Contentment

From Success to Contentment. My original purpose in agreeing to reflect on and disclose aspects of my life was to shed some light on how "success" might evolve and be maintained in the aging process. However, in reflecting on my life, I came to realize that for me, it was even more important to also focus on the life experience of "contentment." Questions kept gnawing at me more and more. For example, what do others say about contentment? What might success mean? What might be the relationship between success and contentment? How might contentment develop and persist? How might personality growth and maturity be related to success and contentment? Or what implications might some of these factors have not only for the individual person but also for people in leadership positions who influence many? What does research have to say about all these questions?

Instead of contentment, others have used words like "inner freedom" (May, 1999), "joy," "peace" or "fulfillment," (Lama and Tutu, 2017), "meaning in life" (Frankl, 1959; 1966), "self-actualization" (Maslow, 1954), "life satisfaction" (Seligman, 2002), and "happiness" (Chade-Meng-Tan, 2012; van der Merwe, 2014) to convey what appears to be a similar experience.

Happiness gets used even more frequently, especially in more popular and political verbiage. For example, in U.S. political history, our founding fathers' vision for America included the "ideals of life, liberty, and the pursuit of happiness" to reach a more purposeful life (Cunningham, 1987; Fortin, 2019). Of all the terms, I prefer contentment as most relevant and precise.

Although success was very important to me during most of my adult life, now that I am retired, success is generally relegated to the background. I now realize that the inner feeling of contentment about life is much deeper, taking precedence over any such externally defined successes. This should not be taken to mean any lives I may have touched, personally or professionally, nor contributions I may have made are not significant. Rather, I have come to experience all of it in a very different way.

Over the years, I have discovered one must learn not only from one's successes, but also from one's failures and mistakes. Only by experiencing failures can one know success.

Meanings of Success. I have come to believe the word "success" for many, especially in our American culture, is mostly defined by achieving money, power, and fame, usually within a very materialistic framework. If people make such successes a direct goal for themselves, it appears they can easily fall prey to never having enough or always seeing someone else as having more, a never-ending cycle. By never having enough, any such successes experienced are likely to feel transitory and superficial, thereby breaching a stabilized contentment experience.

In contrast, if success is mostly defined by focusing on goals that bring "good to others" or emphasize the "greater or common good," I've found the psychological conundrum can be avoided. In that way, any money, power, and fame achieved are experienced secondarily as a by-product of one's own inner desire to bring "good to others for the common good." This golden rule (men and women for others) perspective can keep one focused on doing good for others rather than just for oneself. Such a process requires learning genuine compassion for others, in other words, looking past oneself to others on a sustained basis.

Competitiveness. Such an evaluation also requires a person learn how to manage their own and others' feelings of competitiveness, especially if they are intense. Not doing so could keep the focus solely on selfish needs. More mature ways of handling competitive drives should be studied and learned (Greenberg, 2011). In such ways, one might begin earning an inner, more pervasive experience of contentment, while still achieving success.

Coping with Pain. I have also learned that earning such enduring inner feelings of "contentment" can require the psychological capacity to cope with pain. In general, one can "go" through pain or "grow" through pain. Contrary to much healthcare and pharmaceutical marketing, all pain is not to be avoided by automatically prescribing or consuming pain medications. Developing a reasonable tolerance for pain is part of a necessary psychological maturing process. Pain experienced during traumas in one's life can paradoxically provide the opportunity to learn things about oneself. It is the organism's way of saying to you "something is wrong that needs attention."

Therefore, pain is not all bad and can serve a productive motivational role for an individual. Unfortunately, there are no "deep pockets" to advocate for such a position, counteracting the extensive advertising by the healthcare and pharmaceutical industries that pain should be avoided. Of course, there is a place for pain medications, but rather, they are currently being overprescribed, some are too addictive, and, overall, the drugs are available too easily.

The reliance on heavy pain medications also correlates significantly to the havoc of addictions, such as the current opioids epidemic, frequently beginning with legal prescriptions for heavy pain medication. Once addicted, many of these persons go to heroin and/or fentanyl use with an increased probability for an overdose. Opioids, including heroin, are greatly addicting with estimates up to 40 percent of occasional users. A medical director friend of mine once stated: "...with all the addicts I have treated over the many decades, never once did a patient say or imply, 'Gee, doc, I wanted to become an addict.'" Addictions are truly psychopathological.

Health professions are beginning to again understand the positive value of patients learning how to develop pain tolerance and coping skills. They butt heads against an enormous profit motive incentivized by pharmaceutical companies to continue pushing pills for everything, especially strong addictive pain medications such as opioids, based on the tacit assumption that all pain should be avoided.

Growth and Maturity. From a different perspective, growth or maturity requires us to experience ourselves as both separate and differentiated from others, while still being very much a part of a connected, living humanity. It also requires us to be empathically connected with others who are experiencing disproportionate suffering and pain, including people outside our immediate family/social connections.

Experts tell us that loving, authentic concern, empathy, and the capacity to focus beyond oneself on others are required for such growth and maturity (Maslow, 1973, 1974; Masterson, 1985; Elson, 1987; Rowe and Mac Isaac, 1989; McWilliams, 1994). Such maturity helps unify different people through empathic understanding (altruism in its highest form) rather than dividing people due to differences, especially when such differences are based on misinformation, lies, fear, anger, or other negative feelings.

In reality, some people do not develop reasonable levels of maturity and self-growth for a variety of reasons. They may not even be aware of the need or care about it. If they acquire power, fame, and/or wealth in our society, it can be at the expense of suffering to others, due to a propensity to be self-oriented and selfish.

Leadership Roles. If in private or public-sector leadership positions, such persons will generally devalue or ignore responsible social values, such as being compassionate and other-oriented, while tending to devalue social justice issues. Instead, they are likely to function in a more primitive, Darwinian, survival of the fittest, win-at-all-costs attitude, emphasizing primarily their own more selfish needs at the expense of others. For example, in business, they are likely to see employees and/or stockholders, investors, or consumers as commodities rather than persons, thereby manipulating them for self-gain.

The self-centered leader generally has an exaggerated sense of self-importance and tends to see the world only through their own, materialistic eyes. Making money is experienced as the only "real" motive and source of their identity. An extreme example of this type of selfish, exploitative leader (or person) is reflected as a common theme in the TV show, "American Greed" (CNBC). Similar examples of such persons could be pointed out in other positions in other areas of work life, not just business.

A More Positive Note. I believe most leaders are reasonably mature and compassionate, but they too can revert to more Darwinian modes of leadership practice, tending to gloss over their effect on others, thereby creating suffering for many persons.

A remedy for this type of business dynamic is frequently reflected today in another somewhat popular TV series titled "Undercover Boss" (CBS; CNBC). In the show, a CEO disguises his/her executive identity and physically "works" among a few frontline employees in the organization, getting to know them on both a personal and employee level, discovering their organizational commitments and strengths while simultaneously learning about their personal suffering and struggles. The disguised CEO's eyes are frequently opened empathically to such an employee as a person, frequently including the employee's personal and financial suffering. Most importantly, the CEO will frequently bring about meaningful solutions for the suffering of those employees. This is good. I frequently wonder whether the CEO finds similar solutions for a large organization's many other committed employees who may also exist and be suffering? If not, more discovery and compassionate problem-solving need to occur.

On a positive note, more theories for effective 21st century corporate, educational, and sport leadership models (Garfield, 1986; McFarland, Senn, and Childress, 1994; Janssen, 2007; Gore, 2013; McNair, Albertine, Cooper, McDonald, and Major, 2016) are shifting from an emphasis on skills relying on position, authority, and power (self-oriented traits) to include skills emphasizing relationships and influence (other-oriented traits), defining leadership and "peak performers" (Garfield, 1986) as values-based and even exploring inner or deeper levels of balance within the leader (Kucia and Gravett, 2014).

The same concerns might similarly be raised within the political arena as politics frequently reflect differing values in leadership styles. At one extreme, some political leadership models promote considerable nationalism, divisiveness, polarization, and selfish forms of leading, while at the opposite extreme, other political leaders emphasize more globalism, altruism, acceptance, and unification of diversity with empathy, including programs which act as a safety net for the more vulnerable marginalized members of society.

On a fictionalized U.S. presidential level, these two extreme opposite forms of political leadership are exemplified by the self-centered, corrupt, and cruel President Francis Underwood in the TV series, "House of Cards" (Netflix) and, in two different TV shows, the socially responsible and high-integrity President Tom Kirkman in the TV series, "Designated Survivor" (ABC; Netflix) and President Elizabeth McCord in the TV series, "Madame Secretary" (CBS; Netflix).

If you have an interest in films and have not viewed these three series, I would strongly recommend each, especially to focus on the two very different types of extreme leadership personalities and styles.

From yet a different perspective regarding how different paths can lead to being elected to political leadership positions, one can also become familiar with the provocative research findings why people tend to vote the way they do for political leaders (Westen, 2007). Many voters are frequently influenced strongly by conditioned feelings they experience about the candidate. If they are conditioned to like and trust them, they usually vote for them. If they don't trust and/or like them, they don't vote for them. Unfortunately, an understanding of the political policies the candidate proposes is, at times, secondary.

The unscrupulous social manipulator knows trust for a candidate can be intentionally broken much easier than earning trust for a candidate. Breaking trust can be achieved by a person or group who intentionally provides misinformation and/or lies in a systematic manner about a candidate that can be instantaneously sent via mass-media to targeted peoples, many of which will pass on to others the misinformation and lies concerning the targeted candidate. This process can be repeated in many ways over time with the effect of influencing millions of peoples' attitudes first, then with many ultimately their beliefs and voting behavior.

Specific procedures were identified in detail in the 2016 presidential election favoring Trump over Clinton, conducted by a number of Russian operatives, articulated in Volume 1 of the Mueller Report (Mueller, 2019), a legal investigative study incorporating legal rules of collecting evidence. The specific methods they used were outlined. Indictments of many specifically named operatives also were made, even though court hearings are unlikely since they are in Russia. Nevertheless, others have been indicted and imprisoned. Unfortunately, not many people have incentive to read the Mueller Report. The legal report is reduced by some to political fodder rather than kept on a legal investigative level, a very highly dogmatic thinking style. "I do not need to read it, I already know what it says... nothing, just biased."

Changing Attitudes and Behaviors. Being a specialist in behavioral science, including knowing well the effects regarding group dynamics, if I had adequate resources, I could develop such an effective team and procedures to change many persons' attitudes first, then behavior (voting) next, by using misinformation and lies. That would assume I had no ethics and was not concerned about possibly breaking the law.

Nevertheless, it could be done. If you don't believe ethical systematic programs are effective, much less unethical ones, just ask yourself, why are corporations willing to pay multiple thousands of dollars for brief systematic TV spots if advertising didn't change behavior? Add to TV spots the use of mass digital communications, it becomes even more powerful if done systematically.

Nevertheless, it may be fair to conclude, if more inclusive, other-oriented, value-based leadership models do become more widespread, more individuals, organizations, and societies will likely benefit with less propaganda, not only with greater possibilities for achieving success, but an opportunity for greater dignity and contentment among many more of its members/citizens.

Relationship of Success and Contentment. Permit me to make some final observations regarding possible distinctions between success and contentment. Maybe, success can be defined more by achieving single goals or satisfying particular acts, whereas contentment may require accumulated personal "successes" over time. The goals to be accomplished with aging may need to be across different areas of personality, such as within the physical (health), financial, social, intellectual, and spiritual areas. For example, by having reasonable health and/or building a reasonable financial foundation for your retirement, you might ideally be more easily able to focus on higher-level goals for success, thereby discovering greater contentment, life satisfaction, and self-actualization through achievements in virtually all areas of retirement life.

Success also appears to have more of an external recognition by others associated with it than does the experience of contentment. In other words, others can more easily observe, define, and measure your successes as opposed to your inner experiences of contentment. Remember, contentment is not likely sustainable without success, but success appears possible without contentment.

Failure also occurs as we pursue success. Major mistakes and failures will occur along the way; that is part of being human. Learning from those mistakes and failures is most important. Taking charge and, when necessary, responsibility for those mistakes and failures is also important, while demonstrating the capacity to move on constructively with your life. At the same time, it is important to mend any injuries, especially social ones, within yourself and others as best you can for the continuing buildup of more stable experiences of contentment.

Although most major Eastern philosophical, religious, and spiritual traditions speak about contentment as a cornerstone to wellbeing (Cordaro, 2016), I am not familiar with many Western psychological descriptions or studies that examined much about the experience of contentment.

Life satisfaction studies might be the closest (Seligman, 2002). Perhaps the lack of research is not entirely an oversight.

As I reflect on my life, I can remember many instances of consciously seeking success, but find it difficult to remember many efforts of trying to reach contentment. Maybe I am not alone in that experience. Our Western culture emphasizes achievement and material success, not contentment. In Western culture, we are typically not taught to give much consideration to the experience of contentment.

In popular speech, we are told to seek happiness, but technically, happiness can't be sought as a goal in itself. It can only be experienced as a byproduct of achieving a goal. I believe it should be limited to being a situational feeling state. Such feeling states can't be sustained. If one is sad, one can't be happy, but one can still be content. Our American culture unintentionally overgeneralized and idealized the definition and description of the experience of happiness while generally ignoring the experience of contentment.

As a result, contentment appears to become more significant, less compartmentalized, more pervasive and psychically structuralized only as certain successful life experiences mount over time. With aging, contentment may be discovered more persistently as a part of one's total self, rather than only in reference to certain life "successes." Overall, we might learn greater insights about contentment from the wisdom found in Eastern cultures.

More systematic research needs to be pursued about contentment in order to clarify the nature, conditions, social-cultural factors, and possible developmental aspects of the experience.

In Summary. Finally, let me run through some aspects of contentment in the following way: Success does not guarantee contentment before or during retirement, but is necessary for our contentment. One can be content while not only being happy, but sad. One can be content in good health, but also in less than good health. One can be content when one is financially secure, but also when financially anxious. One can be content when one's personal relationships are loving, but also when they include frictions. One can be content when ambiguity exists in one's mind as well as when significant questions seem answered and settled. Some can be content with a belief in God, some lacking such a belief. The inner experience of contentment is somehow earned and discovered, both through one's successes and failures, but not guaranteed.

Bottom line, within the confines of any developed measures of contentment, all such issues appear amenable to empirical study for further clarification. Others will need to specify through research how the experience of contentment becomes an enduring part of our retirement lifestyle.

CHAPTER 12
Retirement

Meanings of Retirement. I believe the word "retirement" has many more practical meanings today than in the past. Until the past couple generations, death was not uncommon about the same time, if not before retirement. To consider it a stage of life would not have applied to most. Only during the past several generations has it become a last stage of life for many as longevity has increased.

One's station in life helped determine what choices became possible during retirement. My generation was one of the first to have the possibility of greater retirement options for more people. Future generations will likely continue to have the opportunity to plan for retirement options, although for many, under different conditions. I believe it would be foolish for today's younger generations not to plan and develop such long-term goals.

Perhaps retirement for many might be defined as leaving one lifestyle to enter another. It would not imply "sitting on a couch or rocking chair" or any other type of passive lifestyle unless demanded by severe disability. Additionally, it may not remain as solely a late-life experience.

If the world population continues increasing significantly, there may not be anywhere near the number of jobs available to keep up with the number of people potentially employable. Advances in technology, especially robotics, artificial intelligence, and globalization will likely continue to eliminate many jobs that exist today, but will they also add more jobs? If new jobs do not keep pace, planning for how people live and meaningfully spend their time during earlier times in life (mini-retirement or re-tooling periods when younger) may present totally new problems for individuals and societies to solve.

Such periods of temporary unemployment in life may require individuals and societies to find new ways for larger portions of the population to experience, not only safety and security in their lives, but also dignity in how they spend their time, both at work and otherwise. Solutions such as working anywhere from a four-hour workweek (Ferriss, 2009) to a four-day workweek might occur for more people.

Or the notion of work and maybe retirement itself may need to be redefined. For example, retirement might be limited to when a person has reached a point in their life when they either can't continue working due to physical or psychological impairments or, when aged, they choose to turn their life toward different active goals no longer including their previous paid employment.

During earlier ages in the life cycle, people will also likely struggle with the necessity of making vocational changes (learning new skills) in their work lives on a more frequent basis than ever before. Increased time gaps (mini-retirements or time-outs) may occur in periods of such vocational and market change, leading to possible episodes of vocational confusion, instability, and identity issues, unless such experiences become more normalized and integrated into people's work, play, and educational lives. Informed visionaries are already speculating about such possible changes in societies.

I was fortunate to spend my 45 years of post-training work life in, mostly, a very stimulating university environment (and network of universities) with many great administrators, faculty, staff, alumni, and students.

I was able to fulfill many separate goals consulting in numerous clinical, educational, health care, judicial, law enforcement, political, religious, sports, and corporate organizations. On the level of policy development and management, I was able to serve in administrative and numerous elected executive positions within local, state, and national professional psychological organizations.

These varied opportunities, including international experiences, permitted me to actualize many of my work (administrative, clinical, supervision, and teaching) goals. Psychological and interdisciplinary research studies, along with the opportunity to advise and mentor numerous graduate students in their theses and dissertation research studies regarding all types of human behavior with people from all walks of life, also kept me in touch with a much wider range of knowledge and "other real-world experiences" of people.

My personal goals with my family experiences were very satisfying overall, even though not always ideal. I was still able to discover success and contentment.

Finally, my entrepreneurial interests and activities were supported and successful more times than not. Having a number of good mentors and other continuous support systems was extremely important along the way. I can't fully express my gratitude. My professional practice and investing acuities were successful because mentoring was available when needed.

Retirement has been conceptualized as consisting of different stages. Spector and Lawrence (2018) list five stages of retirement, beginning with a stage of anticipation going into retirement, going through a honeymoon stage in early retirement, experiencing a period of disenchantment, then discovering a stage of rejuvenation, and finally experiencing fulfillment.

Unfortunately, not everyone experiences much of the fourth and fifth stages due to a lack of successful planning for retirement. As a result, stress, anxiety, and depression can develop, including a greater probability of developing a variety of lethal illnesses, malignant neoplasms, cerebrovascular issues, Alzheimer's disease, influenza, and pneumonia, etc. The natural antidotes to all of this deterioration are education and effective planning.

Final Comments About Retirement Planning. Planning can be conducted by employing very specific procedures (Spector and Lawrence, 2018), sometimes referred to as "how-to" models, to more open planning models developed in different ways. I observed people utilize different methods based on their own preferences for how to go about planning. Moreover, special programs with supplemental readings are beginning to offer greater options for retirement planning. Finding agreeable and trusting persons to meet and discuss retirement issues can also lead to a very productive outcome.

The worst of all choices is to do nothing, leaving retirement issues up to fate. I would further add that preparing only financially would leave a huge void in discovering a meaningful, full retirement experience. A word to the wise, be proactive. If you are one of the "lucky" ones to reach retirement years, enjoy your final years with earned success and contentment.

CONCLUDING REMARKS

This last stage of life may provide the ultimate time and opportunity for many older persons in our culture to reflect on their life experiences and become more aware of their earned contentment. As an oversimplified metaphor, achieving an experience of underlying contentment can be similar, in part, to what happens when one learns to scuba dive—another former hobby of mine.

When on the surface of seawater, one can experience turbulence from the waves, being thrown around, finding it uncomfortable and anxiety-provoking, even leading to seasickness, thereby keeping you focused mostly on your anxieties and fears. In contrast, you quickly learn to experience calm and inner satisfaction once you sufficiently submerge beneath the turbulent surface, permitting yourself to more easily focus on events, circumstances, and life around you.

In a similar way, the inner or deeper experience of enduring contentment in life can be realized much more easily by focusing within ourselves on our inner, deeper, other-oriented goals which can make more bearable the surface turbulence of seeking successes in everyday life, even if the turbulence occasionally reaches tsunami levels.

Maybe all these life lessons can even make it easier to ultimately accept and not be anxious or fear death, life's true final stage. At my age, I can now more easily accept death as part of the natural process of life. When the time arrives, my final challenge will be to have the courage and opportunity to die with dignity, my final lesson to model for others, especially family. After all, death is the final challenge in life to learn to accept and maybe even welcome, rather than solely feeling resigned to it or resisting it (Kübler-Ross, 1974; 1975). As the renowned psychoanalyst Erik Erikson (1950) wisely observed: "...healthy children will not fear life if their parents have integrity enough not to fear death."

Do I consider my aging process "successful?" Certainly, I feel very fortunate to have discovered in retirement a reasonable underlying and pervasive inner experience of contentment, including an inner peace and experience of dignity. For me, contentment is now more pronounced and psychically structuralized than the experience of success. Nevertheless, crises continue to occur on occasion and my life is not always "happy" or "joyful," but it is content.

Being old is not always easy as the body wears down and losses continue to mount. What I am stating is that even during such experiences, contentment can persist. It is also supportive and consoling to know some others report similar life experiences. At the same time, it is distressing to realize that others struggle, sometimes immensely, with their life experiences. The only comfort is knowing we are all part of the same connected humanity.

I know of no immediate solution other than empathic kindness, a compassionate helping hand, and remaining active in an age-appropriate manner. The long-term solution is likely related to educational goals, learning to effectively teach "life strategies" (McGraw, 1999; Ferriss, 2009) and "awaken the giant within" (Robbins, 1991), not to mention learning how to realistically negotiate the data-based forces operating in this world (Gore, 2013). If a person is struggling with inner feelings of contentment, it brings to mind the thought, "There, but for the grace of God, go I."

But, maybe not entirely, if a fair amount of effective preparation, education, and self-awareness is thrown in as well.

Maybe, in some ways, it all boils down at this point in at least my life to being able to answer the following question in a positive manner. Overall, do I believe I have given and continue to give it my best try in leading a value-based life for myself and others? During earlier stages of life, asking myself that same question would not have seemed as relevant, even though it was still as important to answer. Currently, my response incorporates the pervasive feelings of contentment, joy, and life meaning I experience.

For some older readers, my hope is my life story might help them to develop more clarity for integrating and ultimately comprehending better their own life travels. For some younger readers, I hope to aid them in developing a more practical roadmap leading to retirement regardless of the specific personal and vocational directions they pursue.

Roadmaps for life's journey can be based on many different perspectives or "starting points." For example, my roadmap relies primarily on a starting point based on a very pragmatic psychological analysis using self-examination and reflection across developmental and different life areas.

One could also use different starting points, such as from American history. One can begin with the insights from our founding fathers by using their writings as a tool to develop a roadmap for discovering purpose in one's life journey (see Ch. 5 and Appendix A, in particular, Fortin, 2019). Alternatively, one could also use a starting point based on a belief in God's revelation, to develop a roadmap for living one's life (Meissner, 1992; 2001).

Finally, I must admit, there is a part of me that also wonders, might there yet be in my life more substantial materials to supplement a couple of these chapters? I hope so! Maybe what I am really discovering is one's life journey is not over till death closes the portal!

Now, it is your turn to do your own psychological self-examination of your life, assuming you decide to work on the challenge. If you do, I believe you increase the likelihood of experiencing greater success in life and discovering greater insights and contentment in your retirement years. Also, I do hope you find the process enjoyable overall.

REFERENCES

Adorno, T.W., Frenkel-Brunswik, E., Levinson, D.J., and Sanford, R.W. (1950). *The Authoritarian Personality.* NY: Harper.

American Psychological Association. (2017). *Stress in America.* Washington, D.C.: https://www.stressinamerica.org

Andersen, K. (2017). *Fantasyland: How America Went Haywire.* New York, NY: Random House.

Bartlett, B. (2017). *The Truth Matters.* New York, NY: Penguin Random House.

Bieliauskas, V.J. and Hellkamp, D. (1973). Four Years of Training Police in Interpersonal Relations. In Snibbe & Snibbe (Eds.) *The Urban Policemen in Transition* (pp. 507-522). Springfield, IL: Thomas.

Bieliauskas, V.J. (1981). Personal communications. Xavier Univ.

Bloom, A. (1987). *The Closing of the American Mind.* New York, NY: Simon and Schuster.

Brokaw, T. (1998). *The Greatest Generation.* NY: Random House.

Chade-Meng-Tan. (2012). *Search Inside Yourself.* NY: Harper.

Collins, F.S. (2006). *The Language of God.* New York, NY: Simon and Schuster.

Cordaro, D. (2016). *Project Contentment.* Director, Yale: https://www.danielcordaro.com

Cunningham, N.E. (1987). *In Pursuit of Reason: The Life of Thomas Jefferson.* New York: Ballantine Books.

Dewey, J. (1910). *How We Think.* Boston: Heath & Co.

DiPuccio, M. (2017). *Live Life for Others.* Unpublished letter.

Dorfman, L.T. (1997). *Professors Talk About Retirement.* Iowa City: University of Iowa Press.

Elson, M. (1987). *The Kohut Seminar.* New York, NY: Norton.

Erikson, E.H. (1950). *Childhood and Society.* New York, NY: Norton. p. 233.

Ferguson, K. (2012). *Stephen Hawking.* New York, NY: Palgrave MacMillan.

Ferriss, T. (2009). *The 4-Hour Workweek.* New York, NY: Random House.

Foer, F. (2017). *World Without Mind.* New York, NY: Penguin.

Fortin, R. (2019). *How the Ideals of America's Founders Lead Us To Purposeful Living.* Cincinnati, OH: Cincinnati Book Publishing.

Franco, C. and Lineback, K. (2006). *The Legacy Guide.* New York, NY: Penguin.

Frankl, V. (1959). *Man's Search for Meaning.* Boston: Beacon Press.

Frankl, V. (1966). Self-Transcendence as a Human Phenomenon. *J. of Humanistic Psychol.,* 6 (2), 97-106.

Freud, S. (1939). *Moses and Monotheism.* New York, NY: Knopf.

REFERENCES

Friedman, T. (2016). *Thank You for Being Late*. New York, NY: Farrar, Straus, and Giroux.

Garfield, C. (1986). *Peak Performers*. NY: Avon Books.

Greenberg, M. (2011, Sept 23). How to keep your cool with competitive people. https://www.psychologytoday.com/blog/the-mindful-self-expression.

Gore, A. (2013). *The Future*. New York, NY: Random House.

Hailstones, T. (1969). Personal communication. Xavier Univ.

Hawking, S. (1996). *A Brief History of Time*. New York, NY: Bantam Dell.

Hawking, S. (2009). *The Universe in a Nutshell*. New York, NY: Bantam Dell.

Hayes, C. (2012). *Twilight of the Elites*. New York, NY: Broadway Paperbacks.

Hayes, C. (2017). *A Colony in a Nation*. New York, NY: Norton.

Hellkamp, D. (1990). The Ohio Multidisciplinary Training Consortium. In D.L. Johnson (Ed.), *The Service Needs of Seriously Mentally Ill: Training implications for Psychology* (pp.139-141). Washington, D.C.: American Psychol. Assoc.

Hellkamp, D. (1993). The Cincinnati Consortium: Training for Services to Seriously Mentally Disabled Adults and their Families. In P. Wohlford, H.F. Myers, & C. Callan (Eds.), *Serving the Seriously Mentally Ill* (pp. 137-142). Washington, D.C.: American Psychol. Assoc.

Hellkamp, D. (1993). Severe Mental Disorders. In G. Stricker & J.R. Gold (Eds.), *Comprehensive Handbook of Psychotherapy* Integration (pp. 385-398). New York, NY: Plenum.

Hellkamp, D. (1996). A Multidisciplinary Collaborative Management and Consulting Model: The Inner Workings and Future Challenges. *J. of Educ. And Psychol. Consultation,* 7(1), 79-85.

Hellkamp, D. (2012). Graduate Commencement Address. Xavier University, CD Format: Cincinnati, OH.

Hellkamp, D. (2017a). Part 1 Success Factors and the Aging Process: https://www.div17oasig.wordpress.com/ American Psychol. Assoc.

Hellkamp, D. (2017b). Part 2 Success Factors and the Aging Process: https://www.div17oasig.wordpress.com/ American Psychol. Assoc.

Janssen, J. (2007). *The Team Captain's Leadership Manual.* Cary, NC: Winning the Mental Game.

Jaynes, J. (1982). *The Origin of Consciousness in the Breakdown of the Bicameral Mind.* Boston, MA: Houghton Mifflin.

Kelly, M. (2012). *The Four Signs of a Dynamic Catholic.* Hebron, KY: Beacon.

Kübler-Ross, E. (1974). *Questions and Answers on Death and Dying.* New York, NY: MacMillan.

Kübler-Ross, E. (1975). *Death: The Final Stage of Growth.* Englewood Cliffs, NJ: Prentice Hall.

Kucia, J.F. and Gravett, L.S. (2014). *Leadership in Balance.* New York, NY: Palgrave MacMillan.

Küng, H. (1979). *Freud and the Problem of God.* New Haven, CT: Yale University Press.

Lama, D., Tutu, D., and Abrams, D. (2016). *The Book of Joy*. New York, NY: Avery.

Maddow, R. (2019). *Blowout*. New York, NY: Crown Publishing.

Maslow, A.H. (1973). *The Farther Reaches of Human Nature*. Middlesex: Penguin.

Maslow, A.H. (1954). *Motivation and Personality*. New York: Harper.

Masterson, J.F. (1985). *The Real Self*. New York, NY: Brunner Mazel.

May, R. (1999). *Freedom and Destiny*. New York, NY: Norton.

McFarland, L.J., Senn, L.E., and Childress, J.R. (1994). *21st Century Leadership*. New York, NY: Leadership Press.

McGraw, P.C. (1999). *Life Strategies*. New York, NY: Hyperion.

McNair, T.B., Albertine, S., Cooper, M.A., McDonald, N., and Major, T. (2016). *Becoming a Student-Ready College*. San Francisco, CA: Jossey-Bass.

McWilliams, N. (1994). *Psychoanalytic Diagnosis*. New York, NY: Guilford Press.

Meissner, W.W. (1992). *Ignatius of Loyola: The Psychology of a Saint*. New Haven, CT: Yale University Press.

Meissner, W.W. (2001). *Life and Faith*. New York, NY: Barnes and Noble.

Mercier, H. and Sperber, D. (2017). *The Enigma of Reason*. New York, NY: Barnes and Noble.

Mersch, C. (2006). *Images of America: Norwood.* Chicago, IL: Arcadia.

Mueller, R.S. (2019). *Report on the Investigation into Russian Interference in the 2016 Presidential Election Vol I and II.* Washington, D.C.: U.S. Department of Justice.

Posey, R.B. (1960). *American Government.* Patterson, NJ: Littlefield.

Robb O'Hagan, S. (2017). *Extreme You.* New York, NY: Harper.

Robbins, T. (1991). *Awaken the Giant Within.* New York, NY: Simon and Schuster.

Rokeach, M. (1960). *The Open and Closed Mind.* New York, NY: Basic Books.

Rowe, C.E. and MacIsaac, D.S. (1989). *Empathic Attunement.* Northvale, NJ: Jason Aronson.

Seligman, M.P., (2002). *Authentic Happiness.* New York, NY: The Free Press.

Sobieralski, A. (May 6, 2011). *An Ode to Dr. Hellkamp.* Unpublished Poem.

Spector, A. and Lawrence, K., (2018). *Your Retirement Quest.* Cincinnati, OH: Cincinnati Book Publishing.

Stern, E.M. and Marino, B.G. (1970). *Psychotheology.* New York, NY: Newman Press.

Stibich, M. (2019). *Sexual Activity Among Older Populations.* Updated October 09, 2019. Google.

Stoll, S. (2017). *Ramp Hollow.* New York, NY: Hill and Wang.

Strauss, V. (2016). Many Americans Know Nothing About Their Government. www.washingtonpost.com/news/answer-sheet/wp/2016/09/27.

Sweeney, P.J. and Fry, L.W. (2012). Character Development Through Spiritual Development. *Journal of Consulting Psychology*, 89-107.

Toffler, A. (1971). *Future Shock*. New York, NY: Bantam.

Toffler, A. (1981). *The Third Wave*. New York, NY: Bantam.

Toffler, A. (1990). *Powershift*. New York, NY: Bantam.

Traister, R. (2016). *All the Single Ladies*. New York, NY: Simon and Schuster.

Traister, R. (2018). *Good and Mad*. New York, NY: Simon and Schuster.

Van der Merwe, P. (2014). *Lucky Go Happy: Make Happiness Happen*. reach@webstorm.co.za: Reach Publishers.

Vance, J.D. (2016). *Hillbilly Elegy*. New York, NY: Harper.

Vedantam, S. (2010). *The Hidden Brain*. New York, NY: Random House.

Wallace-Wells, D. (2017, July 10-23). The Uninhabitable Earth. New York: *New York Magazine,* pp. 24-31. nymag.com.

Westen, D. (2007). *The Political Brain*. New York, NY: Public Affairs.

Williams, J.C. (2017). *White Working Class*. Watertown, MA: Harvard Business Review Press.

Zucchero, R. (2017). Personal communication. Xavier Univ.

Read, learn, and be inspired to plan.

APPENDIX A
Live Life for Others

(An Eighth Grade Project, 2017)
Michael DiPuccio, grandchild

The greatest and most important lesson that my grandpa and grandma taught me was that the most important parts of life are you get a good education, try your best in every situation, help the less fortunate, and take care of everyone and everything. If you miss any of these things, you will never be able to truly know the meaning of life.

My grandpa was a professor of psychology at Xavier University, and his life was focused on making sure that when the students who left his classroom knew all they needed to know about what he was teaching so they could go out, serve others, and make the world better. My grandpa still does some consulting for them, even though he retired. Every time I am leaving Cincinnati to come back home to Cleveland, when we are saying our goodbyes, he always tells me that he loves me, to try my best in school, and to study hard. After hearing it so many times, it truly has an impact on my life.

Whenever my family goes to Cincinnati, my grandma is always there and asking us what we need. Whenever I need something, she is always there to help me out. I'll even tell her that I can get it, but she will insist on getting it. That is just the type of person she is. She married my grandpa knowing just how big of a family he had, but she didn't care. She treats all of us as if we are her real grandkids, and we treat her as if she is our real grandma.

In conclusion, my grandparents taught me a valuable lesson that I will never forget. I learned from them that life's too short to be selfish. I strive to live and be like them as I grow up and as I make a difference in the lives of others.

APPENDIX B
An Ode to Dr. Hellkamp

(A Poem as a Farewell to a Xavier University Career)
April Sobieralski, May 6, 2011
Fourth Year Doctoral Student

Dr. Hellkamp is the man of the hour,
And not a moment too late, we wouldn't want him to sour.
He's been at Xavier for innumerable years,
And his departure from here will cause many tears.
Dr. Stukenberg tried to honor him at our grad student meeting,
But already Dr. Hellkamp's presence is fleeting.
So, we'll give a send-off from the 4th year class.
We're sweet, but you know, we gotta add a little sass.
When we walked in to psychopathology class our first semester of grad school,
We were paralyzed by fear and thought, "Man, I'm a fool!" Dr. Hellkamp spewed his wisdom all over the place
And dang, that PDM took up a lot of space!
We quickly learned that Dr. Hellkamp can do more than just teach.
He's a supervisor, a consultant, does *something* with basketball, and he can also preach.
He's taught us a lot about psychology and about life,
He's a mentor, offers guidance, and support with our strife.
He has shown more care and compassion for his students than anyone I've ever met,
And I know his influence on others isn't over yet.
I know I'm grateful for all the ways he's inspired me

And I bet he'll be there to consult with us in the future (for a small fee)
We wish you the best in your retirement from teaching,
And always remember, your knowledge, your commitment, your impact is far-reaching.

Congratulations on your retirement!

DEDICATION AND ACKNOWLEDGMENTS

This paper is dedicated to my wife, Susan Wideman, and her family, especially Kathy Wright and Paige Wideman, the former like a sister I never had, and the latter as another daughter. I love our Sunday grill-out routines with my daughter Jeannette, including the associated weekly chatter, but, mostly, the love and support. I love our family get-togethers on holidays and other special, sometimes spontaneous, occasions.

The dedication of this paper is also very much directed to all my other grown children and their significant others: Jeff and [Mary J-M]; Joe [J] in memory; Jeannette [JM]; Julie and [Dominic J-D]; James and [Jenny J-J]; and Jon [JH].

Then there is the next generation. From Jeff and Mary, Tom, wife Kristen (T-K), Amy (A), Craig (C), Lisa, husband Ryan (L-R), and Jill (Ji); from Joseph, Sean, wife Heidi (S-H), and Mark (Ma); from Jeannette, TBD; from Julie, husband Dominic, Dominic Jr.(Jr), Mat (M), Sophia (S), Michael (Mi), Armand (Am), and Lena (L); from James, wife Jen, Briana (B) and Olivia (O); from Jon, the triplets, identical Jonah (Jo) and Tanner (T) with their womb-mate, Charlotte (Ch).

Finally, the generation of great-grandchildren include so far; from (T-K), twins Brody and Cooper, and Gabriella; from (C), Ethan; from (S-H), Miah; from (L-R), Riley.

Although beset with a blended family complexity, my family makeup is generally very loving, caring, tightly bonded, and usually supportive. I am very proud of their accomplishments and the values they have incorporated.

I am sure it was not always easy having a psychologist as a patriarch. If not, you each covered it well. My greatest gift from each of you is the love and support I currently feel. I have usually felt support during both my times of joy and times of crises, as well as more balanced times. I hope I have done the same for you.

Blending families is not easy, especially when the family is so large. I believe most everyone has given it their best shot and continues to do so. I can't begin to express my gratitude for how my wife has developed a very strong bond with all the "kids," and vice-versa. Thank you all.

Read this paper, if you will, with respect and interest. Hopefully, it leaves you with more than the musings of an old man, father, grandfather, great grandfather, or, maybe even later, with multiple greats as the generations continue to procreate.

A special thanks to John Getz, Ph.D., a retired English professor, Emeritus, at Xavier, for his selfless time and professional suggestions in reading and helping edit the paper. Similarly, a special thank you to Sue Ann Painter, Vice President and Executive Editor, Tony Brunsman, President and CEO, and Alaina Stellwagen, Associate Editor, at Cincinnati Book Publishing for their valuable suggestions, advice, and support on this project. Finally, to my "sister" in-law, Kathy Wright, for her diligence in picture-taking along with my stepdaughter, Paige Wideman, for her creativity in providing the design and layouts for the book cover.

Without mentioning other names, I dedicate this paper to all my students who have provided both challenges and insights throughout my professional career. Finally, I dedicate this

DEDICATIONS AND ACKNOWLEDGMENTS

work to my many other friends and colleagues at Xavier, to my breakfast groups, discussion groups, book club, brothers, and other family members. A special shout out to all who have provided other suggestions over the many months.

It seems appropriate to bring up a mental game that a number of my friends and I played in the past. It involved asking everyone playing, if you had one wish for yourself and it could involve anything at all, whether seemingly possible or not, what might it be?

Perhaps not surprisingly, my wish would be to be able to somehow come back to life for maybe a couple months every 30 years or so, just to "see" how family and life in all forms have changed. Will the "free world" continue to expand or contract as democracies? Will the world continue to avoid a nuclear war? How will the current forces of advancing technologies, globalism, and the environment be playing out in the world? Will effective ways of monitoring facts from fake news be developed? How will my family members, future family members, and students all be doing?

Of course, these would only be a sampling of questions to be answered. Needless to say, my curiosity and desire to learn remains strong!

What would be your wish?